UNDERSTANDING YOUR RIGHTS

Understanding Your Rights

Your Rights and Responsibilities in the Catholic Church

Russell Shaw

CHARIS

Servant Publications
Ann Arbor, Michigan

Published by Servant Publications
P.O. Box 8617
Ann Arbor, Michigan 48107

Cover design by Gerry Gawronski/The Look
Text design by Janice Hendrick/Good Visuals

94 95 96 97 98 10 9 8 7 6 5 4 3 2 1

Printed in the United States of America
ISBN 0-89283-776-4

Contents

ACKNOWLEDGEMENTS

While many individuals and published sources helped me in the writing of this book, I wish to express special thanks to Dr. Germain Grisez, Flynn Professor of Christian Ethics at Mount Saint Mary's College, Emmitsburg, Maryland. His help has been of two kinds.

First, as the text that follows makes clear in many places, I have drawn heavily on his works for my treatment of some of the central themes of the book, including the views on law and morality, rights and obligations, and personal vocation presented here. Especially helpful have been the two published volumes of his masterwork, *The Way of the Lord Jesus: Volume One, Christian Moral Principles* (Franciscan Herald Press, 1983); and *Volume Two, Living a Christian Life* (Franciscan Herald Press, 1993).

Second, Dr. Grisez generously read the manuscript of the book and offered many important criticisms and practical suggestions that have been incorporated into the text. Needless to say, I take responsibility for the final product.

The translation of Scripture used here is the Revised Standard Version, Catholic Edition. The translation of the documents of the Second Vatican Council is *The Documents of Vatican II*, Walter M. Abbott, S.J., General Editor; Very Rev. Msgr. Joseph Gallagher, Translation Editor (Guild Press, 1966).

ONE

A Charter for the Laity

HERE ARE TWO VERSIONS of the challenges and opportunities that confront Catholic lay people as members of the Church. First: "Pray, pay, and obey." Second: "The newness of the Christian life is the foundation and title for equality among all the baptized of Christ.... Because of the one dignity flowing from Baptism, each member of the lay faithful, together with ordained ministers and men and women religious, shares a responsibility for the Church's mission."

Who knows where the first comes from? For a long time now, much too long in fact, "Pray, pay, and obey" has been a cynical summary of the passive, put-upon role supposedly assigned to the Catholic laity.

The second passage comes from an "apostolic exhortation" of Pope John Paul II called *The Lay Members of Christ's Faithful People (Christifideles Laici)*. Published in 1989 in response to a 1987 World Synod of Bishops that focused on the theme of the laity and their role in the Church and the world, it presents both a rich theological portrait of the position occupied by lay people within the communion of faith and an exciting invitation to them to participate actively in the Church's essential work—continuing the redemptive work of Jesus Christ.

These two visions of the rights and responsibilities of lay people could hardly be more different.

The first assumes that the Church is divided into two radically unequal groups—"unequal" not just in numbers but also in dignity.

At the top of the heap is a tiny elite corps composed of pope, bishops, clergy, and religious (viewed as if they were a kind of clerical auxiliary). The members of this elite group run the show—they make the decisions and cause things to happen. Apostolic initiatives originate with them and are largely their responsibility to carry out. They may be authoritarian and domineering in style or, especially in the years since the Second Vatican Council, they may operate with a lighter, more pastoral touch. It hardly matters: either way, they're in charge.

The second group, at the bottom of the heap, is the laity. Whatever role or status they may have in other spheres of life, as members of the Church they are, and are meant to be, passive and subordinate. "What is the province of the laity?" a British monsignor quipped back in the nineteenth century, "To hunt, to shoot, to entertain?" Lay people are expected to receive the sacraments, keep the rules, support the Church, and do what they're told. Not only did many Catholic laity of the past seem to think of themselves that way. Even today, it seems, many more or less still do.

That is easy to illustrate.

If you are anything like me, you've probably been in many meetings, both formal and informal, at which a group of lay people were discussing some practical question well within their competence: how to organize a fundraiser for the parish school, how to put together an appealing adult catechetical program, or how to approach a pressing community problem from a Christian perspective. A priest enters the room. All eyes turn his way and someone says: "What does Father think we should do?"

The point is not that the priest's input isn't important or shouldn't be sought. In fact, his contribution is needed and valued. But should "Father" always have the final word on matters about which lay people know as much as, and sometimes more than, he? Apparently many Catholics take it for granted that he should.

A document prepared for, but never considered by, the First Vatican Council (1870), helps explain why that is so: "Christ's Church is not a society of equals as if all the faithful in it had the same rights; but it is a society in which not all are equal. And this is so not only because some of the faithful are clerics and some laymen, but especially because in the Church there is a power of divine institution, by which some are authorized to sanctify, teach, and govern, and others do not have this authority."

Certainly that is true in a real sense. Just as certainly, it is not the whole story.

But times have changed—in this case, very much for the better. The change could hardly be clearer than it is in words of Pope John Paul II in his 1989 document on the laity.

Citing the gospel parable of the laborers in the vineyard (Mt 20:1-16), he says all members of the Church are equal in their dignity as Christians. This equal dignity in turn "guarantees and fosters the spirit of communion and fellowship and at the same time becomes the hidden dynamic force in the lay faithful's apostolate and mission. It is a dignity... which brings demands, the dignity of laborers called by the Lord to work in his vineyard." That is a giant leap forward from the view prevailing a century earlier.

It is important, though, to grasp the fact that, seen in historical perspective, the "new" view of the laity and their role is also very old. From the beginning, the Church had a hierarchical structure, with real authority and powers of governance vested in its clerical leaders. But there also existed a lively grasp of the diversity of roles, offices, functions, and charisms belonging to her various members, including lay people.

How did the Church manage not just to survive but to spread and grow in the hostile environment of the Roman Empire during the early Christian centuries? How did she weather both the sneers of pagan sophisticates and recurring bloody persecutions? To be sure—because God willed it so and the Spirit saw that it should happen. In human terms, however, this remarkable, and otherwise hardly explicable, development also had a lot to do with the laity and their self-understanding.

A famous Christian document, "The Epistle to Diognetus," written around the year 200 A.D., says of the Church's ordinary members: "Yet while they dwell in both Greek and non-Greek cities, as each one's lot was cast, and conform to the customs of the country in dress, food, and mode of life in general, the whole tenor of their way of living stamps it as worthy of admiration and admittedly extraordinary.... What the soul is in the body, that the Christians are in the world.... Such is the important post to which God has assigned them, and they are not at liberty to desert it."

As a summary of the how the Catholic laity are meant to view and live out their rights and responsibilities as members of the Church, that can't be bettered even now.

ABOUT THIS BOOK

Throughout much of the twentieth century the Catholic Church sought to capture—or recapture—a true and positive view of the role of her lay members. This effort had many important stages. But by far the most important was the Second Vatican Council (1962-65).

The Council's agenda was much too broad for anyone realistically to claim that it was "about" the laity. Still, the bishops gave a central place to laypeople in their deliberations and their documents. Several of these latter stand out for what they have to say about the laity.

The Constitution on the Church (Lumen Gentium) embodies an understanding of the community of faith as a "people"— hierarchically organized, to be sure, but marked by her members' fundamental equality in dignity and by their shared responsibility for accomplishing her mission of extending Christ's redemptive work. Its entire fourth chapter is devoted to the laity, while chapter five sounds a universal call to holiness—a call "to the fullness of the Christian life and to the perfection of charity" which, the Council makes clear, is directed as much to laypeople as it is to clergy and religious.

The Decree on the Apostolate of the Laity (Apostolicam Actuositatem) focuses specifically on lay men and women and their diverse tasks as Christians. And *The Pastoral Constitution on the Church in the Modern World (Gaudium et Spes)*, scanning the signs of the times, deals with a social situation in which the primary responsibility for bringing the gospel message to bear upon contemporary problems resides with laypeople.

Since Vatican II, in short, there can be no doubt that, according to the Church's official teaching, the laity have many serious obligations and rights arising precisely from the fact that they *are* members of the communion of faith.

FROM THEORY TO PRACTICE

But how could this insight be translated from the level of theory to the realm of practice? One critically important step was taken in 1983, with the publication of the revised Code of Canon Law for the Western (Latin) Church. Among the points *New Code* of the new Code, highlighted by Pope John Paul II in a document accompanying its publication, is its treatment of "the duties and rights of the faithful and particularly of the laity."

Book II of the Code entitled "The People of God" contains an entire section devoted to "The Obligations and Rights of All the Christian Faithful" and another specifically covering "The Obligations and Rights of the Lay Christian Faithful."

My intention in this book is to discuss the rights and responsibilities of Catholic laypeople as they are enumerated in these two sections of the 1983 Code of Canon Law. Not that other parts of the Code don't have a lot to say to and about the laity—they do; but the heart of its vision of laypeople is contained here.

At the same time my approach is deliberately nontechnical. Readers looking for a technical commentary on canon law will have to look elsewhere. I simply wish to identify the rights and responsibilities of the laity contained in the Code of 1983 and to explain in general terms some of what they imply and why that is important. In order to make sense of the explanation, certain other matters pertaining to the Church and the laity, as well as to matters like law, rights, and duties, must also be covered. In a nutshell, that's the book.

Here and there throughout I shall make reference to a mythical Holy Family Parish. It goes without saying that this is a literary device, intended to tie certain themes together and bring them down to earth. There is no real-life Holy Family Parish—unless, of course, it is a bit like them all.

"But," someone might object, "isn't what you're describing too narrow an approach? Anybody glancing at the Code of Canon Law can see that it doesn't cover—doesn't even *pretend* to cover—all the responsibilities and rights of laypeople. Why not look at this question in a broader perspective?"

The objection makes an important point. The 1983 Code does not come close to exhausting the rights and duties of laypeople. For one thing, it does not attempt to present a comprehensive treatment of human rights and responsibilities in general but instead sticks to duties and rights *in the Church*. For another thing, it leaves many aspects of rights and responsibilities even in the Church untouched or open to further development.

Here it is necessary to call attention to another limitation of this book arising from the Code of Canon Law itself. Neither the Code nor my treatment of it provides a manual of conflict resolution within the Church; neither sets out a well-developed system for judging and settling disputes. This may be regrettable, but it's a fact.

Moreover, it isn't clear that any alternative would, here and now, be an improvement. We live in a time when people are quick to haul one another into a court to settle their quarrels. It would not be helpful, to say the least, to contribute to the creation of a parallel situation within the community of faith. Ours is a Church, after all, not a small claims court. And after saying everything that needs saying about canonical rights, due process and the rest, the imperative for Christians is to exercise mercy, forego their rights, forgive one another, and seek reconciliation. That also is one of the central points I am trying to make in this book. I hope it does not come as a grave disappointment to any reader. I consider it basic and indispensable.

But still it is useful and important to focus on the laity's "rights and responsibilities" as they are found in the Code of Canon Law. Taken together, they add up to a remarkably positive vision of the role of laypeople. Furthermore, not only does the Code say many things which are important in their own right, but the very fact that it says them is a breakthrough of great importance. Why that is so becomes clear from a glance at history. The 1983 Code has roots—antecedents—and it is important to know something about them in order to grasp its significance.

A TALE OF TWO CODES

The 1983 Code of Canon Law had a predecessor: the famous Code of 1917. A remarkable achievement in many ways, the earlier legislative compilation helped guide the Church successfully for well over half of an exceptionally turbulent century. But it also had gaps and limitations. Nowhere are these now more clear than in its treatment—or, more accurately, its failure to treat—the rights and responsibilities of laypeople.

There were 2,414 canons in the 1917 Code. ("Canon" comes from a Greek word, *kanon*, meaning rule, norm, or measure. It has been the term used for Church laws for many centuries.) Out of all these canons, however, hardly any deal with the laity, and these few mainly in relation to marriage questions.

This omission itself makes an eloquent statement. Regarding the time the 1917 Code of Canon Law was being drafted, one writer has remarked, "There existed neither a theology of the laity nor any of the phenomena which, moved by the Holy Spirit, were to manifest themselves within the Church in eminently lay types of Christian life." Or, more bluntly: "The 1917 Code failed to pay adequate attention to the laity precisely because it would have been impossible to do so."

A lot happened in the Church, as it did in the world, between 1917 and 1983. As we have seen, far and away the most important thing for the Church's understanding of the Catholic laity was Vatican Council II. The 1983 Code of Canon Law cannot be understood and appreciated apart from the Council.

In fact, they were linked from the very start. On January 25, 1959, at the Roman Basilica of St. Paul Outside the Walls, Pope John XXIII announced that he intended to convoke an ecumenical council—a gathering of all the bishops under the leadership of the Pope. But he also announced something else. He planned to establish a pontifical commission to revise the Code of Canon Law.

For practical reasons, the Council had to come first. Only as it was drawing to a close did the project of revising the Church's law get underway. As it did, Pope Paul VI, who had succeeded Pope John XXIII, underlined the connection between the Council and the Code. Canon law, he told the first plenary session of the commission responsible for revising it, "must be accommodated to a new way of thinking proper to the Second Ecumenical Council of the Vatican, in which pastoral care and new needs of the people of God are met."

HOW ARE THINGS IN HOLY FAMILY?

So this book concerns matters of enormous importance. The Second Vatican Council presented a new charter for the Catholic laity. The 1983 Code of Canon Law casts that charter in terms of canonical rights and responsibilities. To the best of our abilities, we all need to understand what it says.

There is plenty of evidence that many Catholics today do not have a good grasp of their duties and rights as members of the Church. The problem is not just that they haven't studied canon law; it is that, to varying degrees, they have become confused about what it means to be a Catholic.

That also is a reason for this book. Discussing the rights and responsibilities of lay Catholics may not clear up all the urgent questions about "Catholic identity" vexing the Church in the United States today. But the questions never will be resolved unless and until American Catholics adopt a much clearer view of their membership in the Church than many now seem to have.

To a great extent, the questions boil down to this: In any particular place, how can we tell whether the decisions of the Second Vatican Council are on the way to being carried out? I once put that query (rather casually, I'm afraid) to a priest with much pastoral experience. His answer was more than I'd bargained for.

How do we know if we're on the right track or not? The question is simpler if we consider a single parish.

It is on the right track because its people are praying more. An increasing percentage receive the sacraments frequently and devoutly. There are more generous acts of charity among them. The people, especially the children, know the Church's teaching on faith and morals. The liturgy is conducted according to the Council's norms, with fervor and decorum.

The priests are dedicated, spiritually minded, and sure in their faith. There are vocations. The parish is marked by fraternal charity and an effective concern for the poor. And we must also include consultation with the laity, an ecumenical spirit, and the spirit of evangelization. Obviously I have a fairly traditional set of criteria, but I think my criteria are those of the Council.

Is the Church ever on the 'wrong' track in a particular area? How would you know? I think the only answer can be by conformity or lack of conformity with the rule of faith, which eventually involves conformity or lack of conformity with the See of Peter. Evidently, there are places in the Church today where a great deal of confusion exists. And where people are confused enough, how can they even know what the right track is?

As a summary of rights and responsibilities properly understood and put into practice (or else not understood and not put into practice) that will do quite well for the moment. And the painful fact is that the prescription sketched out by my priest friend is rather widely ignored, even violated, in the United States at the present time.

Polls and personal observation both make it clear that many American Catholics either do not know very clearly what the Church teaches on many matters of faith and morals or else reject it. The same is true of many matters of Church discipline.

Sunday Mass attendance and reception of the Sacrament of Reconciliation or Penance have plummeted. Abortion and divorce rates among Catholics approximate the rates among the general population. Vocations to the priesthood and religious life are down sharply, producing a growing shortage of priests and the virtual disappearance of women religious in some areas. And there is, to say the least, no particular evidence that many Catholics in public life—or in the professions and secular pursuits generally—are notable for seeking to apply gospel standards to secular affairs. The "split between the faith which many profess and their daily lives" that the Second Vatican Council declared to be "among the more serious errors of our age" seems to be set in Catholic concrete.

Still, that's not the whole of it.

Talking with a knowledgeable American bishop who was present as an observer at a gathering of European bishops in Rome several years ago, I made some of the usual remarks about the difficult situation of Catholicism in secularized Western Europe: declining Mass attendance; declining priestly and religious vocations; widespread acceptance of a consumerist, hedonistic, essentially pagan moral code. His reply was illuminating: "Certainly that is true—the numbers are down. But I think those who still work at their religion are better Christians than they used to be. It isn't easy to be a Christian in an environment like this. You have to try harder, and trying harder means you do a better job."

The same thing may be true of the Catholic community in the United States. Faced with serious challenges to religious practice, not a few Catholics have made a stronger Christian commitment than before. As a result, they have grown in depth and maturity of faith.

But the overall picture is hardly encouraging. Consider the results of a 1992 Gallup survey of Catholics (commissioned and released, be it noted, by several Catholic groups which dissent from much Catholic teaching and discipline). Here are some of the disturbing statistics: 67 percent favored women priests; 87 percent agreed that the Church should "permit couples to make their own decisions about forms of birth control"—an ambiguous question, obviously, but the response pretty clearly indicates support for contraception; 70 percent agreed that Catholics in good conscience can vote for political candidates who support legal abortion; 52 percent said abortion should be legal in many or all circumstances.

Not surprisingly, the survey found that support for positions like these was stronger—sometimes substantially so—among Catholics who never or seldom go to church. But on other matters—contraception is a notable example—it turned up no significant difference between the views of weekly Mass-goers and the rest.

It can't reasonably be argued that this situation is what Pope John XXIII had in mind when he convened the Second Vatican Council or what the Council itself envisaged. Pope John XXIII and the Council looked for the emergence of a well formed, highly motivated laity, committed to Catholic doctrine and practice, who would shoulder the task of evangelizing the world in the name of Christ and his Church. In many places today, however, the secular world is doing more to "evangelize" Catholic laypeople than they are doing to evangelize the world.

HOW WE GOT WHERE WE ARE

What explains the difficult situation of the Church in the United States? No doubt there are many contributing factors, but two causes in particular stand out.

Theological and practical dissent in the Church in the years since the Second Vatican Council explains part of the problem. Most Catholic laypeople are not theological specialists, but they do read the newspapers and watch television, and the spectacle of theologians and others publicly defying the teaching authority of the pope and bishops has had a profound effect. Indeed, so have the inroads of dissent in the Church's own pastoral programs and educational institutions. Many observers, for example, have fretted that certain Catholic colleges and universities are seemingly "Catholic" in name only, while making an ostentatious point of being independent from the Church's teaching authority.

The result of all this, quite simply, is that many people now believe that it is possible to be a "good Catholic" without accepting Catholic teaching. Pope John Paul II took note of that attitude in a talk to the U.S. bishops gathered in Los Angeles during his 1987 pastoral visit to America. He called it a "grave error" that challenges their teaching office.

Something else with a profound impact on the Catholic laity also has been going on. Assimilation—the movement of Catholics into the political, economic, and cultural mainstream—has occurred at an accelerating pace.

No doubt this process of assimilation represents progress in many ways. Catholics in the United States are on the whole much better educated and far more affluent than their immigrant forebears were. Catholics in large numbers are present in the professions, the academic world, and political life. Catholics have clout.

But we've paid a price for it.

American Catholics in recent decades were becoming part of a secular culture whose beliefs, moral values, and standards of behavior were at the same time moving into increasing conflict with Catholic beliefs, values, and standards on many issues of personal morality and public policy.

Dissent and cultural assimilation have reinforced each other, even while exerting a powerful influence upon Catholics. For it is just those issues where dissent has been most intense—sexual morality, divorce and remarriage, abortion and so on—that also have been central to the revolution in values altering the moral landscape of secular society. Consciously or unconsciously, dissent has provided many people with a rationale for joining this revolution with relatively few qualms of conscience.

RIGHTS, RESPONSIBILITIES, ... AND CLERICALISM

In addition to cultural assimilation and dissent, however, there is another factor—not so often noticed but no less powerful—that helps to explain the present troubled state of the Church and, especially, confusion about the laity's role. It is clericalism—the view that clerics are and ought to be the dominant, active members of the Church.

Clericalism has been a reality in Catholic life for many centuries. The reasons for that are complex; we'll examine them a bit later. Historically, too, the clericalist mentality has expressed itself in different ways in different times and places. In Europe, for example, it contributed in past centuries to over-involvement by clerics in secular politics—a long and extremely tangled story in its own right—which in turn gave rise to the violently anticlerical movements of the eighteenth, nineteenth, and twentieth centuries.

Thanks to the provisions of the First Amendment to the United States Constitution and to the painful lessons learned from Europe, that pattern of clericalism and anticlericalism has never been particularly strong in America. But the clericalist mentality itself is alive and well on these shores.

Note, though, that the "clericalist" mentality of which I speak is hardly limited to priests. In fact, a strong case can be made for the proposition that clericalism now is more prevalent among Catholic laypeople than it is among their clergy! Although it has several sources, the most important of these may be the idea that only priests and religious have "vocations" while the laity, when all is said and done, do not. (We shall see later just what's wrong with that view. It has an important connection with the question of rights and responsibilities.)

In practical terms, the idea that the laity are second-class citizens, religiously speaking, naturally leads to the attitudes and ways of behaving noted above—to the notion that the clergy are and should be the active, ruling class in the Church, while laypeople are and should be passive and subservient ("What does Father think about that?"); to the view that priests and religious are responsible for the Church's evangelizing mission, while laypeople need only stand on the sidelines and watch; to the belief that it is the job of the clerical hierarchy to take the initiative in all things religious and give the orders, while the role of lay men and women is essentially "pray, pay, and obey."

The results, where the laity is concerned, are twofold. Clericalism causes passivity and noninvolvement in some laypeople, alienation and bitterness in others. In both cases it does grave harm to the Church, her members, and her mission.

All of this can be, and sometimes is, expressed in terms of rights and responsibilities. The confusion on this score produced by clericalism runs very deep. It extends from passive indifference on the part of some laypeople to angry rebellion among others.

These days it's not uncommon to hear alienated, embittered Catholics (or ex-Catholics) complain about how the Church "hurt" them by denying or violating their rights in one way or another. I have heard such talk many times. Occasionally, of course, these angry people have real grievances, although the grievances usually concern individual, erring representatives of the Church more than they do "the Church" as such.

But very often, too, such people are angry about having been denied the satisfaction of a "right" that doesn't really exist—that cannot exist because it is incompatible with the divinely instituted order of Catholic life. I mean such things as the "right" to receive the sacraments after divorcing and remarrying without an annulment, the "right" (in the case of women) to ordination as priests, the "right" to have an abortion or to practice the gay lifestyle—the "right" to do any number of things that God's law, taught by the Church, forbids any Catholic to do.

As these examples suggest, the problems of the Catholic

community in the United States will not all be solved by achieving a nonclericalist understanding of the duties and rights of laypeople. There will, however, be no solution without it.

In his apostolic constitution introducing the 1983 Code of Canon Law, John Paul II makes a telling point about the Church's law and what it tells us concerning the obligations and rights of Catholics. The Code, he says, is "in no way intended as a substitute for faith, grace, charisms, and especially charity" in the lives of Catholics. Its purpose is to create within the Church an environment that, while giving first place to "love, grace, and charisms," at the same time "renders their organic development easier in the life of both the ecclesial society and the persons who belong to it."

Christian rights and responsibilities, correctly understood, are embodiments of the love, grace, and charisms of which the Holy Father speaks. Along with a correct appreciation of the Christian vocation (and also of the specific vocations of individual Christians), plus a sound ecclesiology—a true vision of the community of faith to which all baptized persons belong—our rights and responsibilities are keys to understanding, accepting, and performing our specific roles as members of the people of God, the body of Christ, the communion of faith and love which is the Catholic Church. We all need to know them better.

Finally, then, how does our mythical (but fairly typical) Holy Family Parish look in this light? Probably something like this.

Holy Family is a suburban parish, neither too large nor too small, with six hundred or so Catholic households within its borders. There are a fairly large number of families with two or three school-age kids, a good number of older couples whose children have left home, quite a few widows and singles.

The parish is overwhelmingly middle-class and white-collar. Families typically seem to have incomes in the $40,000 to $50,000 range, and many obviously have a great deal more than that, especially where, as almost always is the case, husband and wife both work. Most adults have some college education, over half are college graduates, and lots have graduate or professional degrees. The parish includes quite a few lawyers and doctors, as well as many well-paid middle management types.

There's a parochial school with two nuns (the principal and the second-grade teacher) and an otherwise lay faculty. The school is quite popular in the lower grades, but classes thin out at the seventh and eighth grade levels, as parishioners start sending their kids to public schools or else to other, more prestigious private schools. From early fall to late spring, CCD classes are held in the parish school Sunday mornings from 11:00 to 11:45. Not many children attend.

The pastor, Monsignor Thomas Hellman, has been at Holy Family for twenty years. He's sixty-three, two years short of retirement, a slightly gruff, no-nonsense kind of priest with a somewhat authoritarian style. If not exactly well-liked in the parish, he is at least viewed with respect. The associate pastor, Father Tom Ross, thirty-four, has been at Holy Family for three years. An extrovert and a kidder, he makes up for what Monsignor Hellman lacks in joviality.

Mass attendance has slipped noticeably at Holy Family over the years, but there's still a respectable turn-out for the three Sunday celebrations of the Eucharist (eight, ten, and noon on Sunday morning) and the Saturday evening 5:30 Mass. At Christmas and Easter the church is packed, leading some parishioners to wonder where all those people are the rest of the year. Collections have been dipping as Mass attendance has declined, but Holy Family has no serious financial problems—yet.

A few people go to confession monthly, a large number maybe once or twice a year, and some apparently never. Weddings and baptisms are frequent. Holy Family has the usual complement of parish organizations (CYO, Sodality,

Father Ross' Bible study group, Home and School, Knights of Columbus, CCD as well as a corps of eucharistic ministers and lectors, a choir, and lots of ushers. A relatively small number of parishioners are active in these groups. Most are not.

Holy Family has a "twinning" arrangement with a parish in the inner city, but mostly that only means sending money. There is little or no personal contact. Nor is there much interaction with Protestant or Jewish congregations in the neighborhood. The Catholics of Holy Family have plenty of Protestant and Jewish friends, of course, and intermarriage is common, but ecumenism as such is a moot issue.

Liturgies at Holy Family are decorous but not inspiring. The homilies are earnest but rather bland. No one appears very angry, very excited, very anything. No doubt the parish has its share of quiet saints, but mainly people are merely nice. They neither argue much about their rights as Catholics nor fret much about their responsibilities. You could almost imagine they didn't think much about either.

TWO

What Kind of Church?

TYPICALLY, MOST PEOPLE in Holy Family Parish are unaware that the Catholic Church in 1983 received a new Code of Canon Law. That's a pity. For if some at least dug into the document and started applying it to their lives as Catholics, they would find it an eye-opener.

There is no more authoritative introduction to the 1983 Code than the one provided at the time of its publication by Pope John Paul II. The apostolic constitution *Sacrae Disci - plinae Leges—The Laws of Sacred Discipline*—supplies a compact overview of the laborious process by which the Code was developed, along with a helpful statement of the reasons for this major undertaking.

John Paul II identifies two main purposes for the revision of the 1917 legal code, announced by Pope John XXIII in 1959. Both of these purposes are closely linked to the Second Vatican Council, which "Good Pope John" announced at the same time.

The first purpose is also the fundamental purpose of Vatican II—"the renewal of Christian living." Although it would be easy to dismiss that phrase as a pious, but not very illuminating cliché, that would be a mistake. For, as Pope John and the Fathers of Vatican II saw it, the renewal of Christian living was not a vapid cliché but an urgent necessity—not just in Rome or Buenos Aires or Tokyo but everywhere, including Holy Family Parish.

Quite simply, Christian living—that is, the way in which members of the Church understand their "membership" and seek to live it out—had to be renewed if the Church was to have any hope of effectively carrying on its divinely assigned mission in and to the modern world. This, after all, was—as it emphatically still is—a world which in recent centuries has drifted ever further away from religious faith and gospel norms, with increasingly disastrous results for humankind. On the eve of the twenty-first century, that problem and its consequences remain as grave as ever.

Pope John XXIII did not convoke the Second Vatican Council merely to engage in ecclesiastical housekeeping. Nor did the members of the hierarchy who labored at Vatican II's four arduous sessions from 1962 to 1965 see it that way. The bishops sought to lay the theoretical groundwork for significant practical changes in the day-to-day life of the Church—that is to say, in the lives of Catholics—in order to make the Church a better instrument of God's salvific will.

So, too, with the revision of canon law. The aim was not to tidy up a few loose ends existing among a multitude of ecclesiastical regulations important only to a tiny handful of specialists and scholars. Rather, the project was seen as necessary to provide a legal framework that would help bring to fruition the renewal of Church life inspired by the Council.

But how did Vatican II seek to renew Christian living? That question points to the second major purpose of the revision of the Code as identified by Pope John Paul II.

Obviously the renewal intended by Vatican II extends to many specific areas of Catholic life—liturgy, ecumenism, the priesthood and religious life, the apostolate of the laity, the study and reading of Scripture, missions and evangelization, and much else besides. Underlying what the Council said about all these things, John Paul observes, was Vatican II's "doctrine of the Church."

More than anything else, the Church's understanding of herself was renewed at Vatican II, as the basis and necessary condition for the general renewal of Christian living. In theological language, this ecclesial self-understanding has a special name: ecclesiology—the theology of the Church.

The central document of the Second Vatican Council, upon which the Council's other fifteen documents are based, is the *Dogmatic Constitution on the Church, Lumen Gentium* (The Light of Nations—that is, Christ himself). It is a landmark in Catholic ecclesiology. Of crucial importance to the subject matter of this book, it supplies the essential elements for the new view of rights and responsibilities of laypeople reflected in the 1983 Code of Canon Law (a view that, presumably, ought to be reflected in the conduct of Catholics).

All this points to a conclusion: To understand our duties and rights as members of the Church, we must start with the ecclesiology of Vatican Council II—with the vision of the Church which the Council embraced for itself and commended to the rest of us.

THE CHURCH AS BODY OF CHRIST

"By her relationship with Christ, the Church is a kind of sacrament or sign of intimate union with God, and of the unity of all mankind. She is also an instrument for the achievement of such union and unity. For this reason... this Council wishes to set forth more precisely to the faithful and to the entire world the nature and encompassing mission of the Church."

These words come at the very start of the *Dogmatic Constitution on the Church*. They situate the Church at the center of God's plan for humankind and so also at the center of human affairs.

That is critically important. There are not two separate and distinct "histories" working themselves out side by side over the centuries, with little or no contact and interaction—on the one side, secular history, what most people are disposed to think of as *real* history, a record of human conflict and achievement, triumph and tragedy; on the other side, something else called "salvation history," a mysterious, invisible, purely spiritual process by which God's will for human beings is realized. In reality, there is only *one* history: the unfolding of God's benevolent plan, even in the face of repeated human blindness and disobedience.

In this one, single historical process, moreover, the Church— "a kind of sacrament or sign" of the union of human beings with God and one another—has a central role. This is an awesome responsibility. It requires much of the Church. First of all, it requires that the Church have a clear understanding of herself and her mission.

Throughout the centuries, of course, the Church has had a self-understanding that, under the guidance and protection of the Holy Spirit, has remained on target in its essentials. But one need not know a great deal about ecclesiastical history to realize that the emphasis and details in the Church's self-understanding have varied enormously from one era to another. (Nor is it any secret that, from time to time, the Church has picked up certain cultural barnacles and administrative anomalies having very little to do with its true nature and role.)

In the course of two millennia, then, the Church naturally has thought of herself in various ways, and has used various metaphors to express these self-understandings. *The Consti-*

tution on the Church recalls a number of these images in its first chapter, entitled "The Mystery of the Church."

In Scripture, for example, the Church is spoken of as, among other things, a sheepfold, a flock whose shepherd is God, a field to be cultivated, and a vineyard (all these are images appropriate to the agricultural society in which the Church first emerged and grew). She also is likened to a building, a temple, a Holy City, a mother, and a pilgrim on the way home to God.

This kaleidoscopic multiplying of metaphors is not surprising. The community of faith which Jesus established is a rich and complex mystery which, moreover, naturally has adapted itself to particular cultural circumstances in different times and places. No single metaphor for the Church tells us everything about her, but each tells us something important to know.

In the last chapter we glanced at the view that prevailed around the time of the First Vatican Council, in the middle years of the nineteenth century (and before and after then, too). The theologian Avery Dulles, S.J., notes that it has a "pyramidal pattern" according to which "power is conceived as descending from the pope through the bishops and priests, while at the base the faithful people play a passive role and seem to have a lower position."

The pyramid version of the Church is much derided today. Obviously, it does have serious disadvantages and limitations. Still, it makes clear something true and important: it expresses the Church's structured, hierarchical nature clearly and forcefully. But in doing so, as we now realize, it leaves out a great deal.

Not surprisingly, then, another way of looking at the Church grew in popularity in the first half of the twentieth century, until eventually it was confirmed by Pope Pius XII in an encyclical published in 1943 (*Mystici Corporis*). "If we would define and describe this true Church of Jesus Christ—which is the holy, Catholic, apostolic, Roman Church," Pope Pius XII wrote, "we shall find no expression more noble, more sublime or more divine than the phrase which calls it 'the mystical body of Jesus Christ.'"

Avant-garde in its day, this way of seeing the Church nevertheless has ancient roots. "Body of Christ" is the image preferred by St. Paul himself and used by him in several of his epistles. For example: "For just as the body is one and has many members, and all the members of the body, though many, are one body, so it is with Christ. For by one Spirit we were all baptized into one body—Jews or Greeks, slaves or free—and all were made to drink of one Spirit... Now you are the body of Christ and individually members of it" (1 Cor 12:12-13, 27).

The *Dogmatic Constitution on the Church* devotes the whole of a long article to the Church as the mystical body of Christ (*Lumen Gentium*, 7). Drawing on St. Paul's teaching, it makes several important points.

The unity of the members of the mystical body—with Christ and with one another—comes from the activity of the Holy Spirit and the effects of baptism and the Eucharist. The Council quotes 1 Corinthians 10:17: "Because there is one bread, we who are many are one body, for we all partake of the one bread." But along with this extraordinary unity there also exists the diversity that one expects to find in any body—"in the building up of Christ's body there is a flourishing variety of members and functions."

The Constitution links the Holy Spirit's activity to both realities, unity and diversity: "There is only one Spirit who, according to his own richness and the needs of the ministries, distributes his different gifts for the welfare of the... Church (cf. 1 Cor 12:1-11)." Preeminent among these gifts are the authority given to the apostles—an authority to be exercised even over "those who were endowed with charisms"—and the bond of charity among the body's members.

"The Head of this body is Christ," the Council declares. All of its members should be formed in Christ's image "until he is formed in them." His members are destined for final fulfillment with him in heaven. But in the meantime: "Made one with his sufferings as the body is with the head, we endure with him, that with him we may be glorified (cf. Rom 8:17)."

Finally, using an ancient and beautiful image, the Council likens the unity of Christ and the Church to the unity of spouses in marriage: "Having become the model of a man loving his wife as his own body, Christ loves the Church as his bride (cf. Eph 5:25-28). For her part, the Church is subject to her head (cf. Eph 5:22-23)."

Seeing the Church as the body of Christ brings out several important truths about this unique community. One of these, as we have seen, is the diversity of offices, ministries, gifts, and functions that are present in this single, united entity. Another concerns its structured, hierarchical character.

Both things are clear in the teaching of St. Paul. For example: "His [Christ's] gifts were that some should be apostles, some prophets, some evangelists, some pastors and teachers, for the equipment of the saints, for the work of ministry, for building up the body of Christ" (Eph 4:11-12). For its part, Vatican II firmly rejects the idea that a hierarchical structure and the mystical body are somehow opposed to each other or can be separated. Far from forming "two realities," it insists, they make up "one interlocked reality"—the Church (*Lumen Gentium*, 7).

If there is a single word which sums up all this for our present purposes, it is *complementarity*. As the different members and their different functions are required for the health and well-being of a human body, so in the "body" of the Church different members have different jobs to do for the good of one another and the good of the whole. This is crucial to a proper understanding of rights and responsibilities. It is crucial to the good health of a microcosm—a cell, as it were—of the universal Church like Holy Family Parish.

THE CHURCH AS PEOPLE OF GOD

While strongly affirming the importance of the image of the Church as the mystical body of Christ, the Second Vatican Council gave special attention to yet another aspect of the Church's understanding of herself: the people of God.

This too has ancient roots. In the Old Testament we see God establishing a covenant with Israel and setting forth its terms in a law binding the people to him and to one another. "Provided that you keep the commandments of the Lord, your God, and walk in his ways, he will establish you as a people sacred to himself" (Dt 28:9). This image of themselves as God's covenanted people is central to the self-understanding of the Jewish people throughout the triumphs and sufferings recorded in the Bible.

Looking ahead to Messianic times, the Old Testament also speaks of a new covenant that God will establish with human beings (Jer 31:31). Vatican Council II identifies the fulfillment of this promise: "Christ instituted this new covenant, that is to say, the new testament, in his blood." He did so, the *Constitution on the Church* says, by calling together "a people made up of Jew and Gentile [and] making them one, not according to the flesh but in the Spirit. This was to be the new People of God."

What does it mean to say that the Church is the people of God? The Council devotes the whole second chapter of the *Dogmatic Constitution on the Church* to considering the implications. They are too numerous even to summarize here, but one point especially stands out. Individually and collectively, the members of this people share in the threefold mission and ministry of Jesus Christ as prophet, priest, and king. That is true not just of *some* of the members—not just Monsignor Hellman and Father Ross of our mythical Holy Family—but of them *all*.

The source and explanation for this remarkable fact are found in baptism. People assembled for a Sunday afternoon christening at Holy Family often think of this sacrament as little more than a social custom—a pleasant, traditional way of celebrating a baby's birth. Others who take a more religious view may focus on some limited aspect of the sacrament. So, in the past, the emphasis was on the fact that it takes away the guilt of original sin. At present, often enough, it is the idea that baptism is a ritual of initiation.

Both things are true, but neither expresses the full reality. Baptism is the foundational sacrament, our rebirth in Christ, whereby we begin to participate in divine life and also to live a way of life not only supported but to a great extent organized by the other sacraments. Here is "membership in the Church" in its fullest sense.

The *Constitution on the Church* presents this view of baptism when it speaks about the people of God. Describing those who are baptized as "a holy priesthood," it says they are able to "offer spiritual sacrifices and proclaim the power of Him who has called them out of darkness into His marvelous light.... Everywhere on earth they must bear witness to Christ and give an answer to those who seek an account of that hope of eternal life which is in them."

So, as a consequence of baptism, all of the members of the people of God—all the people of Holy Family and every other parish, and not just their priests—are meant to participate in the work and mission of the community, which seeks to continue and complete the work and mission of Christ. Traditionally, this is expressed as a threefold mission or ministry: as priest, as prophet, and as king. In describing the people of God, the Council discusses each.

• As Priest: Although the ordained priesthood and the priesthood of the faithful "differ from one another in essence and not only in degree," nevertheless they are "interrelated." How? "Each of them in its own special way is a participation in the one priesthood of Christ." This is expressed in the Eucharist, where the people of God "offer the divine Victim to God, and offer themselves along with

It." It also is expressed in the day-to-day living out of the particular duties of various states in life and vocational commitments, including Christian marriage, through which people respond to God's gifts by living lives of priestly service to God and one another.

• As Prophet: The essential work of a prophet is to proclaim God's love and truth, as God himself communicates them. That also is something every member of the people of God is meant to do, each according to his or her own circumstances and abilities. For some, it takes the form of specifically teaching Christian doctrine; for all it involves the public witness of a Christian life. "The holy People of God shares also in Christ's prophetic office. It spreads abroad a living witness to Him, especially by means of a life of faith and charity."

• As King: The Church, the people of God, participates in the kingship of Christ. But kingship in this context has a special meaning: It involves not temporal power but a ministry of service that orders the life of God's people and aims at unity—above all, the unity of humankind with God. "Among all the nations of earth there is but one People of God, which takes its citizens from every race, making them citizens of a kingdom which is of a heavenly and not an earthly nature... The Church or People of God takes nothing away from the temporal welfare of any people by establishing that kingdom... The Catholic Church strives energetically and constantly to bring all humanity with all its riches back to Christ its Head in the unity of His Spirit."

THE CHURCH IS A "COMMUNION"

In the years since the Second Vatican Council it sometimes has been suggested (or even vociferously asserted) that these two ways of getting at the mystery of the Church—as body of Christ, as people of God—are in conflict. Not only is that idea mistaken, in practice it leads to serious problems.

Liberals, attempting as they see it to "democratize" the Church, have emphasized the idea of people of God, with its leveling thrust that seems to do away with distinctions and set everybody on the same footing. Conservatives have stressed the body of Christ, an image which in their view preserves due respect for office, rank, and authority in the conduct of ecclesiastical affairs.

But there is no real conflict between these two visions of the Church (except, that is, for the unnecessary conflict generated by ideologues of the left and right). Instead of being in conflict, "people of God" and "body of Christ" are complementary ways of understanding the Church. Each says something true and important about this mysterious and multidimensional reality called "Church." Each needs the other if we are to have a rounded picture of the Church as she is.

"Body of Christ," as we have seen, calls attention to the structured, hierarchical character of the Church. This is a body in which different members have different jobs (including jobs like governing and obeying, teaching, and learning). Provided the body is healthy and in good working order, however, there is no conflict—no power struggle—between the different members, but rather a smooth working relationship in which each one recognizes his or her need for the others. Only when the "body" is in poor health do conflicts and power struggles arise.

St. Paul puts his finger on the heart of the matter. "For the body does not consist of one member but of many. If the foot should say, 'Because I am not a hand, I do not belong to the body,' that would not make it any less a part of the body. And if the ear should say, 'Because I am not an eye, I do not belong to the body,' that would not make it any less a part of the body... Now you are the body of Christ and individually members of it" (1 Cor 12:14-27). The members of the Church, including a small part of it like Holy Family Parish, in a real sense *need* each other. They would be incomplete without one another.

As for the "people of God," this image of the Church underlines the equality in dignity of all the members—an equality rooted in baptism that calls each one to active participation in the Church's threefold mission. Today this is absolutely essential if lay Catholics are to have an accurate understanding of how they fit into the life of the Church. It is essential not just for the sake of their self-respect but especially so that, along with the clergy and religious, they will shoulder their share of responsibility for doing the Church's work, from the parish to the level of the universal Church.

As with "body of Christ," however, so also "people of God" is distorted and falsified when pushed to extremes. This has sometimes happened in the years since Vatican II—for example, by ignoring or denying the distinction in kind and not just in degree between the priesthood of the faithful and the ordained priesthood, or by trying to create a politicized "People's Church." The emphasis in speaking of the Church as people of God should always be on "of God." This is a people formed by God—*his* people—that only remains such as long as it abides by his law.

COMMUNION AND COMPLEMENTARITY

The principle needed to avoid the errors of the extreme right and the extreme left is *complementarity*. It also is essential to understanding rights and responsibilities in the Church. Things which are complementary do not conflict. They mesh harmoniously and work together. This is eminently true in the Church.

This principle of complementarity is central to the ecclesiology of the Second Vatican Council. Underlying both "body of

Christ" and "people of God" in the Council's thinking is a notion that sheds light on both teachings and helps make their relationship clear. It is *communio*—the Church as a community or "communion."

Pope John Paul II discusses *communio* at length in his document on the laity. He makes it central to his treatment of the Church and of the role of the laity as her members. A "proper understanding" of both the Church and the laity, he writes, can be found "only in the living context of the Church as communion."

What does it mean to say the Church is a communion? In answering that question, the pope quotes from a document issued by the World Synod of Bishops which he convened in 1985 to review successes and failures in the implementation of the Council twenty years after its close. Declaring that "communion" as applied to the Church first of all signifies communion with God, it states: "The opportunity for such communion is present in the Word of God and in the sacraments. Baptism is the door and the foundation of communion in the Church. The Eucharist is the source and summit of the whole of Christian life... The Body of Christ in the Holy Eucharist sacramentalizes this communion, that is, it is a sign and actually brings about the intimate bonds of communion among all the faithful in the Body of Christ which is the Church."

The pope also quotes the words of Pope Paul VI, the day after Vatican Council II ended: "The meaning of the Church is a communion of saints. 'Communion' speaks of a double, life-giving participation: the incorporation of Christians into the life of Christ, and the communication of that life of charity to the entire body of the faithful, in this world and in the next, union with Christ and in Christ, and union among Christians, in the Church."

Exploring all the implications of this view of "communion" would take us far beyond our present subject. The significance it has for the rights and responsibilities of Catholic laypeople is profound enough. Pope John Paul suggests the framework for considering these latter when he says that communion in the Church is characterized by "a diversity and a complementarity of vocations and states in life, of ministries, of charisms and responsibilities." Because of this diversity and complementarity, he declares, every member of the lay faithful has a "totally unique contribution" to make to the community of faith.

[margin note: diversity + complementarity]

Which is to say: Precisely as a member of the Church, each of us has his or her own Christian work to do. Each of us is irreplaceable in carrying on the mission of the Church, which is the mission of Christ. Ultimately (as we shall see when we come to speak at greater length of vocation and vocations), that is because each has a unique personal vocation, along with the common Christian vocation which comes from baptism and a set of obligations and commitments arising from his or her "vocation" in the sense of state in life.

Obviously, though, there are elements that are common to the vocations of us all. These common elements are our obligations and rights as members of the Church. As Pope John Paul points out in his introduction to the 1983 Code, it is from "the true and genuine image of the Church" that we come to understand the nature and the content of "the duties and rights of the faithful and particularly the laity." It is on this basis that the good people of Holy Family Parish can learn and live the fullness of their identities as Christians called to build up the Church and be of service to a troubled world.

WHY THE CHURCH IS "SHE"

Before leaving this subject of ecclesiology, let's pause briefly to consider another matter. In discussing ecclesial duties and rights it is important not to overlook what is essential: the life of charity animating the Church. I can think of no better way of expressing it than to point out why the Church is called "she."

For a long time I routinely spoke and wrote of the Church as "it." I considered calling the Church "she" to be an instance of the familiar, fussy ecclesiastical rhetoric we'd be better off without.

Lately, though, it has dawned on me that she is the correct pronoun to use in order to express certain fundamental realities concerning the Church. The reasons touch on Christology, the ordained priesthood's special relationship to the Eucharist, women's ordination, and much else, including that life of charity of which I spoke. They directly concern our understanding of the Church herself.

Consider what is implied by always and only calling the Church it. "It" suggests something abstract and impersonal, an entity of an institutional and bureaucratic kind. IBM and the Pentagon obviously are it—no one would dream of calling them she or he. Is the Church in the same category? Calling the Church it suggests that she is.

But there are other and deeper reasons than that for speaking of the Church as she. A familiar text in Ephesians (5:22-32) is crucial here—I mean the one likening Christ's relationship to the Church to the relationship of husband and wife in marriage, an insight prefigured in the Old Testament. Whether or not it makes unacceptable, culturally conditioned assumptions about husbands and wives ("Wives, be subject to your husbands") is beside the point; for, as the writer of Ephesians carefully notes, this passage mainly concerns "a great mystery... in reference to Christ and the Church."

What is this mystery—this truth—about Christ and the Church? Far more than we can grasp, no doubt. But at least the following.

Ephesians calls attention to the fact that Christ stands in a certain relation to the Church and the Church to him. The relationship resembles that of husband and wife. In this covenantal situation, Christ embodies the masculine principle and the Church the feminine. Complementary commitments and

41

obligations of fidelity and love pertain to both.

The image should not be pressed too hard. Christ is ineffably superior to the Church, whereas superiority and inferiority are not (or at least should not be) at issue in marriage. The common element in both cases, however, is the differentiated complementarity of the parties. That common element makes the figure of speech work.

A great deal follows.

For one thing, the situation described in Ephesians underlines a central fact about the Incarnation. The Son of God became Man in two senses: he became a human being and he became a particular human being of masculine gender. The Incarnation means that Christ not only took on generic human nature—he also became an individual, Jesus of Nazareth. He was not only *homo* but *vir*: a male.

That in turn suggests something about the priesthood. In the Eucharist the priest represents Christ. But this is not simply a symbolic representation. It is more correctly described as sacramental. Its reality is expressed by saying that the priest acts *in persona Christi*—in the person of Christ. His action is "his" only in a secondary way and is primarily the action of Christ. The incarnational principle is at work here, too. In fact, we might say, the priest represents Christ as a kind of sacrament of Christ.

That sheds light on the question of ordaining women to the priesthood. In the Eucharist, the priest is in relation to the community gathered for worship as Christ is in relation to the Church. He is, to repeat, a kind of sacrament of Christ. The situation is described metaphorically in Ephesians: Christ-Church, husband-wife, masculine-feminine.

This is not a trivial figure of speech. It expresses the incarnational principle at work in yet another context. And it is difficult—to say the least—to square it with the idea of female priests. It may be that the Christological confusions of the present day have something to do with the growing practice of ordaining women in other Christian denominations as well as with the controversy over the same issue within the Catholic Church. Someone unconvinced that God became Man—in both senses, *homo* and *vir*—is unlikely to have much use for the "incarnational principle" as it is operative elsewhere in the divine economy. Indeed, such a person is likely to consider this a meaningless form of words and an excuse for excluding women from something to which they have a right.

Lastly, then, there is the Church, the community or communion of faith joining its members with God and with one another. To pursue the nuptial metaphor further: Christ's spousal activity vis-à-vis the Church can be expressed by saying that he impregnates the Church with his life-giving Spirit; while the Church for her part conceives and nurtures Christians in her womb by sacraments and the word, until they grow up to the fullness of resurrected life in heaven. "You have been born anew, not of perishable seed but of imperishable, through the living and abiding word of God" (1 Pt 1:23).

None of this adds up to a conclusive argument for or against anything in particular, including refusing priestly ordination to women. But there is nothing unusual about a situation in which we know something to be so without having conclusive arguments to show that it *is* so. In fact, a great deal of reality is not accessible to rational argument or only imperfectly so. Typically, we speak of *seeing* reality, not of reasoning to what is true. Reality is more often grasped by experience and reflection than it is by syllogisms. And the line of reflection suggested above points to a severe tension which, along with the Church's traditional belief and practice in this matter, places a heavy burden of proof on women's ordination advocates.

Finally, let us be aware that there is nothing wrong about calling the Church "it". There are times when it is appropriate (for instance, to bring out the Church's institutional aspect). Indeed, other hallowed metaphors describing the Church, like "body of Christ," require that way of speaking. But she expresses the Church's reality in a very fitting manner: it is a richer, fuller way of pointing to the nature of the Church as a communion and to her relationship to Christ on the one hand and Christians on the other. The Church is the bride of Christ and our mother in the order of charity. The Church is she.

This broadbrush overview of ecclesiology ends very much where it began. The purpose and aim of the 1983 Code of Canon Law, like Vatican Council II, are the renewal of Christian living. The Code's enumeration of rights and responsibilities isn't a dry exercise in legalism. It is meant to help us grasp our vocations and to live them out as members of that communion of faith and charity called the Church. It is as meaningful for the members of Holy Family Parish as it is for the members of the Roman Curia.

But before directly examining the Code, we need to consider a few ideas about law in general and about canon law in particular, in order to dispel some widespread misunderstandings concerning both. That is the purpose of the chapter that follows.

THREE

Understanding Law

A S A MOTIVATOR OF HUMAN BEHAVIOR, law is effective but not very popular. Few people, if any, are wildly enthusiastic about paying taxes but must do so because, among other compelling reasons, the law requires it. In such situations saying "That's the law" is the equivalent of saying, "Do what you're told whether you like it or not."

Confronted with such a directive, people may conform out of a sense of social propriety or simply because they fear the consequences of breaking the law. But coerced conformity does not breed warm and friendly feelings toward law and those who make and enforce it. Saying "That's the law" can come across very much like an impatient grown-up's response to a child who asks, "Why should I?"—"Because I say so." That may settle the matter with children (up to a certain age) but not with adults.

But does this way of thinking about the law amount to a

45

bum rap? In fact, presenting the law and the force of law in this manner misrepresents both.

Good laws do not conflict with human rights but are necessary for their protection. Father Cormac Burke, a civil lawyer as well as a canon lawyer, cites three reasons for this:

1. Rights must be defined in order to be protected, and defining rights is one of the functions of law;
2. those whose rights are violated need a remedy, and supplying remedies for violations of rights also is part of the work of law;
3. rights imply obligations (which are duties to respect rights), and good laws spell out the obligations that some have to respect the rights of others.

This does not make every law a good law. There are such things as bad laws—rules that are out of date or unclear or simply unfair. Instead of protecting rights, bad laws allow some to violate the rights of others: for example, laws that permit abortion and thus violate the rights of unborn human beings.

But even so, law in general is by no means the bogeyman it sometimes is made out to be. A character in Dickens (who himself had extensive, and not always happy, personal experience of the law) declaims, "The law, sir, is a ass." Yet law plays a necessary and usually benign role in human affairs. In the absence of a shared commitment to justice and the laws which are indispensable to making it effective, there is, as St. Augustine says in the *City of God*, "No people... but some kind of mob."

THREE MISUNDERSTANDINGS ABOUT LAW

Misunderstandings about law and its relationship to life are common today. Let us look at three, which are especially widespread. Inevitably, this discussion is bound to seem rather abstract, but it is basic to a sound understanding of our rights and duties as Catholics or, indeed, as members of any community or structured social grouping.

1. Law is the source of morality, and laws are human inventions that can be changed. Thus morality also is changeable, at the discretion of those who make law. This way of thinking about the law jumbles together what is called legal positivism with a highly relativistic view of morality. Regardless of what name or names anyone gives it, however, this attitude undermines law itself. If in the final analysis any particular law is simply *my* idea of what *you* should do, it is possible that you will obey the law—out of conformity or fear—but it is highly unlikely that you will respect it or put your heart into obeying it. In fact, you're likely to rebel as soon as you get a chance. The famous Justice Oliver Wendell Holmes was a legal positivist, and positivism remains the dominant view of law in the United States today. This helps to account for the famous "activism" of the Supreme Court and other courts which have invented novel new legal doctrines on abortion and other issues in recent decades.

Not only do some serious philosophers tend to think this way about law, but so, typically, do those who preach revolutions of one kind or another. For example, orthodox Marxists consider the laws of capitalist societies to be the creations of the ruling class, imposed by the rich upon the poor in order to support the exploitation of the oppressed by their oppressors. Exponents of theories of "liberation" theology customarily think of the source and purpose of law in such terms.

Others best described as cultural relativists consider laws simply to be expressions of the standards of behavior adopted by particular cultures to suit their needs and convenience and enshrine their biases and taboos. The standards of behavior may make sense for a particular culture; but whether they do or don't, they are essentially subject to change—and indeed should be altered—as circumstances change. Not only law but morality stands on shifting, or at least shiftable, sand. "If those people thought it was right," cultural relativists will (if they're logical) say of some abomination like cannibalism or slavery or human sacrifice, "then no doubt it was right for them." (We can safely suppose that cultural relativists of the future will say the same of legal abortion as it exists in the United States today: "If those people thought it was right for them...").

Of course, the liberationists and the cultural relativists have a point. It would be foolish to ignore the elements of truth in what they say. Laws sometimes are imposed or manipulated by the powerful in order to benefit themselves at the expense of the weak. Laws frequently *do* reflect culturally conditioned, changeable notions of right and wrong: for example, laws in various states that, reinforced by the Supreme Court's notorious Dred Scott decision nearly a century and a half ago, sanctioned and supported the institution of slavery in this country.

But this is not the entire story where morality and law are concerned. The Judeo-Christian tradition holds that there are absolute norms of morality: standards of behavior which do not and cannot change because they are grounded in human nature.

These standards of behavior are not creatures of anybody's arbitrary will but are expressions of moral truth—truth based on the requirements of authentic, integral human fulfillment. The norm that forbids the direct and deliberate killing of an innocent person is one example, and there are many others: for instance, the norm against slavery, the norm against stealing, the norm against polygamy and so on. Human laws that embody and protect such norms are similarly based not on social convention but on truth. Laws that violate such norms cannot be just.

Certainly it is possible for societies to adopt and enforce laws that *do* violate moral truth. But such laws are unjust—they are in a sense lawless laws, even though it may be necessary to obey them for the sake of preventing some greater evil (such as breakdown in respect for law generally).

These confusions about law and morality are quite common today where Church law and moral doctrine are concerned. Many people equate the two things: moral doctrine, they assume, is a product of a legislative process by which the pope or the bishops decide to impose burdens on Catholics at large.

This is clear from the way some Catholics—even good Catholics in a setting like Holy Family Parish—tend to refer to particular matters of moral teaching: the Church's "ban" on contraception, the "ban" on remarriage after divorce (without an annulment), and so on. "Bans" are legislative enactments and, as such, subject to change. The implication is that Church authorities could (and probably should) authorize people to contracept, to divorce and remarry, and so on, if they wished to do so. That the norm against contraception and the norm against remarriage after divorce are statements of moral truth seems not to occur to many people. And so the line, heard rather frequently these days from chip-on-shoulder Catholics: "The Church can't tell *me* what to do!"

If this is a problem for moral doctrine, it is even more of a problem where Church law is concerned. The Church's laws plainly are creations of the Church. Over the centuries, they have undergone many changes. Yet Church law, like any good body of law, is not infinitely plastic. Ecclesiastical laws are meant to express and specify and safeguard truth. How the law does this can be and sometimes is changed to suit changed circumstances. But the truth remains what it is, and the law constantly aims to mirror the truth and make it effective here and now.

Take a fairly simple case. Church law on the question of fasting and abstaining has changed greatly over the centuries, and no doubt it will change again in the future. But laws of fast and abstinence are no more (and no less) than expressions and specifications by the authorized law-givers in the Church of the universal need for penance. Regardless of the precise rules on fasting and abstaining that happen to be in force at any particular time, penance itself always has had and always will have a central place in Christian life. There can be no authentic Christian life without penance.

(There's a common misunderstanding, by the way, to the effect that in doing away with the legal obligation to abstain from meat on most Fridays of the year, the pope and bishops also did away with the requirement to practice penance on Friday. They did not. The relevant papal and episcopal documents call on Catholics to make every Friday a day for penitential practices of their own choosing, as a weekly commemoration of Jesus' crucifixion and death. But people have short memories. At a bishops' meeting several years ago, a member of the hierarchy reminded his brothers of the rules on penance still in force, then asked: "I wonder how many of us in this room get up on Friday and ask ourselves, 'What penance shall I do today?'")

2. A second widespread misunderstanding of law is what is known as legalism—the notion that moral goodness consists mainly, or even exclusively, in precise external conformity to rules. Let us be clear at the start: external conformity to a just law is almost always a good thing. Seldom is there any merit in *not* obeying a just law, while disobeying laws that are unjust or, perhaps, simply irrelevant may be wrong—not least, because disobedience, though conscientiously intended, may give bad example and encourage others to break the law in ways that are not justified. So, for instance, adults who ignore speed limits and other traffic regulations in situations where there is no real risk involved nevertheless can do serious harm by violating the law in front of children and impressionable people.

Legalism, however, means more than just obeying the law. We could say that the essence of legalism lies in external conformity to law, without much else. At bottom, it reflects the attitude that morality means sticking to the letter of law and only that. It is the view of both things, morality and law, characteristic of children and immature persons. Typically, legalists are prone to hair-splitting and the minutiae of strict legal observance.

That is true even—or perhaps especially—where what's at issue is not how to keep the law but how to break it. The question is: "How far can you go?" For example, people of a legalistic turn of mind are likely to fret about how much over the posted speed limit they can drive without attracting the unfavorable attention of the police. (How fast they can *safely* drive, whether over or under the posted limit, apparently is less important to them.)

Catholic legalism has existed for a long time. In contexts familiar to the older generation, Catholic legalists in times gone by were accustomed to concern themselves with weighty questions like how much meat they could eat on Fridays before it became a mortal sin and how late they could be for Mass while still fulfilling the Sunday obligation. (Was a hot dog on the safe side of the line or not? If you came in at midpoint during the offertory—at the pouring of the wine and water, say—did you or didn't you "hear Mass"?)

It is easy to caricature such offshoots of the legalistic mentality, yet in many ways legalism is no laughing matter. Among other things, it encourages the idea that someone who gets "dispensed" from moral requirements that he or she finds burdensome has satisfied not just the law but morality.

Not only in the past did Catholics tend to think that way. "Pastoral solutions" and "internal forum solutions" to marriage cases outside the annulment process that excuse people from living up to clear moral norms taught by the Church bear a strong family resemblance to the legalistic "dispensations" of former times.

Here, too, there's an obvious tendency to equate law with moral truth—to suppose that, in the final analysis, the heart of

internal forum solution as legalism

morality lies in either sticking to the rules or else manipulating them successfully in such ways as the rules themselves provide.

The fact of the matter is just the other way around. Ultimately, a good law is "good" because it is faithful to moral truth. Obtaining an informal, nonofficial dispensation from such a law excuses no one from what truth requires. This is the case, for instance, when a divorced and remarried Catholic receives authorization from a priest to receive Communion even though his or her valid first marriage still exists. On the other hand, although careful external observance of the prescriptions of the law usually is a desirable thing, external observance that does not arise from internally conforming one's heart to moral truth is superficial at best and hypocritical at worst. This may be the case, for example, with someone whose notion of his or her responsibilities as a member of the Church does not extend much beyond Sunday Mass attendance and fast and abstinence during Lent. People who want to avoid legalism will try to obey the law. But, more important, they will try to know, internalize, and live by moral truth.

3. A third false attitude—perhaps the most common of all—views law merely in relation to whatever it is we happen to want: as an obstacle to be evaded or a potential opportunity to be exploited to our own advantage. This way of thinking about law is rooted in individualism. With the possible exception of infants, no one seriously objects to all laws in principle. People have no difficulty recognizing the need and desirability of law when it is a question of compelling others to respect their rights or give them what is due them. Indeed, many observers have remarked on the fact that contemporary America is a society with a overdeveloped enthusiasm for legal processes and litigation—a place where individuals and groups are quick to resort to law in order to protect or promote their interests.

For many people, though, the situation is very different when the force of law falls upon them and they are required to do something—pay taxes, make restitution to others for injuring them or their property, or merely keep off the grass—that they don't care to do. Even the most responsible and law-abiding among us have a deep-rooted craving to do as we please and an equally deep-rooted resistance to letting anybody or anything prevent us from doing it.

But that, of course, is exactly what law often does. Then we are tempted to get angry at the law, while looking for ways either to fight it, evade it, or—at best—obey it in as grudging and minimalistic a way as we can get away with.

The spirit of individualism is at work in this attitude. It plays an important part in American culture and the character of many Americans. It is seen in heroic, semi-mythical figures like the frontiersman, the pioneer, the cowboy and, of course, the "Rugged Individualist." Basically, individualism means looking out for number one—putting *my* interests first, ahead of everybody else's, and making sure that my own needs and wants are satisfied before, or even in place of, the needs and wants of others.

It does not follow that other people necessarily are unimportant to an individualist. On the contrary, other people often are very important, precisely to the extent that the individualist has need of them in order to get what he or she wants—physical or emotional gratification, wealth, prestige, whatever it may be.

Not uncommonly, too, individualists manifest real benevolence toward family, friends, and others who provide them with the security and success they desire. But such benevolence is deeply tinged with *self*-interest: The individualist cares about others more for his or her own sake than for theirs.

Typically, individualists are adept at entering into alliance with others of like mind in order to claim their "rights" as an interest group. Such interest groups have little or no real commitment to the common good of the community as a whole. They tend to view social and political life as arenas for power struggles, where they strive to manipulate policy and law for their own benefit and that of similar groups who are their coalition partners, at the expense of other individuals and groups. On the current American political scene the working alliance of radical feminists and "gay rights" groups is a striking example of this.

The phenomenon as it now exists goes well beyond the time-honored political practice of coalition-building in support of good causes. It is far removed from the search for consensus and mutually acceptable compromise. It turns social life into a brutish struggle in which competing interest groups battle one another to get their way.

Individualism's exaggerated emphasis on "rights" has a disastrous impact on efforts to arrive at a sound understanding of law. That is clear, for example, in the case of abortion, where an extreme version of the philosophy of personal autonomy has been taken up even by the Supreme Court.

"At the heart of liberty is the right to define one's own concept of existence, of meaning, of the universe, and of the mystery of human life," Justices O'Connor, Kennedy, and Souter declared in the controlling opinion in a major abortion case (*Planned Parenthood v. Casey*) decided in 1992. But this foggy rhetoric about a "right to define" turns out to signify the "right" to kill the unborn.

It is not surprising that the individualism so widespread in secular culture also finds expression in religious circles. One form it takes is a distorted stress on the role and prerogatives of personal conscience, viewed as a standard of judgment superior to the Church's teaching and law: "I don't care what the Church says about that—my conscience tells me it's all right." Scratch the surface and you may even find that many of the good Catholics in Holy Family Parish think that way, at least on issues like birth control, abortion, and divorce. Monsignor Hellman's and Father Ross' occasional homilies in support of Church doctrine in these areas usually draw privately spoken, negative comments from certain member of the congregation.

Another form is the dreary set of variations on the theme of power struggle marring ecclesial life time and again in recent decades. Indeed, the creation of a "People's Church" at the expense of Church hierarchy is a central goal of some versions of the liberation theology movement. Whatever else might be said of these intra-Church squabbles in the years since Vatican II, they do not arise from a view of the Church as the body of Christ, the people of God, and a communion of faith and charity.

LAW, COMMUNITY, AND THE COMMON GOOD

In place of false notions about law—and so also about rights and responsibilities, whether in civil society or in the Church— we need a correct understanding of the role that good laws play in human affairs. Of course, this book is not the place for a technical treatise on law. But the ideas that follow may help set things in perspective.

Individualists are correct in thinking that law has an important role to play in the fulfillment of persons and groups of persons. Law can contribute a great deal to human fulfillment or it can get in the way.

But individualists are mistaken in thinking of law merely as an obstacle to be evaded or else as an opportunity to be exploited for their own advantage and that of their friends, interest group, or social class. Good laws help identify and protect the conditions required for real human fulfillment. Law is not the only thing that does this, but it does occupy a central place in organizing and directing behavior along positive and constructive paths in a variety of social relationships.

The mention of "social relationships" calls attention to an important fact. Human beings are essentially social by nature, and people achieve fulfillment (or fail to achieve it) in and through their relationships with other persons. The well-being of others is an element of my own well-being. The Second Vatican Council recalls this age-old principle in its *Pastoral Constitution on the Church in the Modern World*. The human person, it points out, is "a social being," and unless a person enters into relationships with others "he can neither live nor develop his potential" (*Gaudium et Spes*, 12).

Furthermore, despite the contrary assumptions of moral relativism, the terms and conditions of human fulfillment are not arbitrary, not inexhaustibly subject to alteration according to individual preferences or changing social circumstances. "We hold these Truths to be self-evident," the Declaration of Independence affirms, "that all Men are created equal, that they are endowed by their Creator with certain unalienable rights, that among these are Life, Liberty, and the Pursuit of Happiness...." Some such shared vision as this has been the indispensable glue binding together every stable, successful society in history. There is a permanent, unchangeable body of absolute moral truth that is the same for all individuals and societies in all times and places.

Plainly, external circumstances—the physical and cultural and moral environment—can and do change from place to place and time to time. For a contemporary citizen of the United States, "human fulfillment" undoubtedly signifies something different in many ways from what fulfillment meant for a man or woman in medieval Europe or a South Sea Islander of the seventeenth century.

But human nature itself does not change and neither do the essentials of human fulfillment. In every time and place genuine "fulfillment," in respect to the nature we all share, will always mean fulfillment in respect to basic human goods like life, truth, friendship, and religion (the human relationship with God or the Transcendent Other). Also, because human beings are social by nature, fulfillment requires fulfillment for not just the lucky few but, insofar as possible, for the many—indeed, for *all*. The plan or set of norms that must shape and guide human action so that authentic human fulfillment understood in this way will occur is what is known as natural law.

Unfortunately, the idea of natural law is widely misunderstood and rejected in the United States at the present time. In fact, the admission a couple of years ago by Clarence Thomas, a United States Supreme Court nominee, that he subscribed to natural law thinking was greeted with consternation by media pundits and politicians who plainly had no idea what he was talking about. The irony is that the basic premises of natural law regarding human nature are fundamental to the unqualified rejection of human rights abuses which these same pundits and political figures routinely decry.

WHY LAW IS NEEDED

If people were perfect, everyone automatically would know the content of natural law and the requirements of human fulfillment, and would work spontaneously and willingly to bring it about. Even then, of course, certain rules of human devising would be needed to guide cooperative action, but the rules would always be reasonable and everyone would willingly abide by them.

But people are not perfect, and their imperfections make rules—laws—all the more necessary. Simply put, good laws make clear and safeguard the standards of social behavior demanded by the legitimate interests of individuals and groups and the well-being of society itself.

Law is not simply at the service of individuals, though certainly it does serve them. It also is required by the common good of the community as a whole. And, to the extent that society's common good embraces the requirements of human fulfillment, human positive law also should express the principles of the natural law. Tax laws, to take only one conspicuous example, ought ultimately to be grounded in a vision of a just society. As such they should give particular emphasis to promoting the well-being of the family and other entities that embody crucial goods of the human person and society.

The idea of the "common good" has a long and honorable history, yet it is not well understood today. Many Americans, to the extent that they think about the common good at all, probably identify it with whatever a majority of people want. The "tyranny of the majority" doesn't faze them—provided, of course, that they are a part of the majority.

Vatican II, however, defines the idea this way: "The common good embraces the sum of those conditions of social life by which individuals, families, and groups can achieve their own fulfillment in a relatively thorough and ready way" (*Gaudium et Spes*, 74). In other words, the common good of a community is the sum of the shared purposes for whose sake people join together to constitute that community—"life, liberty, and the pursuit of happiness," in one familiar formulation.

The Council points out (though it hardly needs pointing out) that a commitment to the common good is definitely *not* compatible with a merely individualistic morality. Instead, it says: "The obligations of justice and love are fulfilled only if each person, contributing to the common good, according to his own abilities and the needs of others, also promotes and assists the public and private institutions dedicated to bettering the conditions of human life" (*Gaudium et Spes*, 30). Good laws are necessary to bring this about.

THE LAW OF THE CHURCH

What about the Church's moral doctrine and its body of laws? In general, what has just been said about human fulfillment, natural law, and the common good applies here, too.

Still, when speaking of the Church, we have to keep in mind another crucially important fact. To the general content of the natural law Christian moral teaching adds the content of *revealed* moral truth—the law of Christ—that includes natural law and adds to it. The natural law remains true and valid, but the law of Christ tells us something more about the terms of human fulfillment within the new covenant with God. It calls us to a higher standard of behavior, and gives us an interior principle whereby we can observe it—the Spirit.

There is an old, and by now rather tired, argument over whether there is such a thing as a specifically "Christian" morality. Indeed, there is. Perhaps its clearest scriptural statement in the New Testament is to be found in the Beatitudes and the Sermon on the Mount, as reported in the fifth to seventh chapters of St. Matthew's Gospel and the sixth chapter of St. Luke. Love of enemies, repudiation of revenge, and even the vindication of one's own rights, strict chastity in mind and heart as well as in external behavior, insistence on the unity and indissolubility of marriage: these things call Jesus' followers to a new, higher standard. Specific norms of behavior reflecting this teaching are scattered throughout the Gospels and the Epistles. The suggestion sometimes made that Jesus did not teach a body of concrete moral truths is evidently not true.

Church law—canon law—does not try to reproduce the entire corpus of Christian moral teaching. It takes this body of moral truth for granted, and attempts to guide behavior within the Church in a way that conforms with it.

Pope John Paul II touches on these matters, as well as on the relationship between the old law and the new, in his introduction to the 1983 Code of Canon Law. He says Jesus "did not in the least wish to destroy the very rich heritage of the law and the prophets" in the Old Testament; rather, he completed it "in a new and higher way" so that it became part of the heritage of the New Testament.

Thus, before we turn directly to the Code itself, it is helpful to conclude this broad overview of law in general and law in the Church in particular by reflecting briefly on what we can discern of Jesus' view of law as it is reflected in the pages of the New Testament. Volumes deservedly have been devoted to this subject. What follows only highlights a few central themes.

JESUS' VIEW OF LAW

What was Jesus' view of law and especially of law's relationship to morality?

Obviously the Gospels don't set out Jesus' philosophy of law, and it is unlikely that, in a technical sense, he even had one. Furthermore, when we find Jesus speaking in the Gospels of "the law and the prophets," as he often does, we should not be too hasty to apply what he says about law literally and inflexibly to the technical complexities of civil law or even canon law. What the New Testament records him as saying on this matter primarily represents his views on "law" in a special sense—the Jewish law, the Law of the Old Covenant between God and his chosen people.

Granted that this is so, however, it is clear from the evidence of the New Testament not only that Jesus had a distinctive view of law but that it is important to his moral teaching. He did not hold any of the false attitudes toward law discussed earlier: legal positivism (man-made law is the source and measure of morality), legalism (moral goodness consists in minute observance of essentially changeable rules), or the notion that law is an imposition on our right always to do just as we please—something either to be evaded or manipulated in our own interests and the interests of friends and allies.

Instead, Jesus taught a morality of the heart, and he insisted that authentic law and law-keeping be an expression of a morality of this kind.

This "morality of the heart" is not a morality of sentiment or subjective feelings. It does not signify that the heart, even if it somehow separates itself from sentiment and feelings, then becomes morality's source. In using this expression I mean that Jesus taught that our choices express what sort of people we are, morally speaking. More than that, our choices *make us to be* people of that sort.

Behavior is important because it puts our choices into action and, for good or ill, causes them to have an impact on other people and the world around us. Good behavior magnifies the goodness of good choices, while evil behavior gives evil choices a social dimension, as it were. Essentially, however, we determine ourselves—as morally good or morally evil—by the choices we make in our "hearts," that is, in the inner core of our moral identity. It is through our hearts, then, that God's moral law enters the domain of the so-called "positive" law of the Church and society.

So, after one of his clashes with the Pharisees and scribes (in the Gospels, repeatedly depicted as embodying a legalistic view of law and morality), Jesus addresses the people in these words: "Hear and understand: not what goes into the mouth defiles a man, but what comes out of the mouth, this defiles a man."

Peter and the other disciples ask him to explain that saying, and Jesus obliges: "Do you not see that whatever goes into the mouth passes into the stomach, and so passes on? But what comes out of the mouth proceeds from the heart, and this defiles a man. For out of the heart come evil thoughts, murder, adultery, fornication, theft, false witness, slander. These are what defile a man; but to eat with unwashed hands does not defile a man" (Mt 15:10-20).

Jesus is not *opposed* to law. He does not take the subjectivist view that moral goodness consists in doing whatever one happens to think is right, provided it is done sincerely and "in good conscience," nor does he share the individualistic notion that law can be set aside or manipulated when convenient. That is *not* his teaching.

Thus: "Think not that I have come to abolish the law and the prophets; I have come not to abolish them but to fulfill them. For truly, I say to you, till heaven and earth pass away, not an iota, not a dot, will pass from the law until all is accomplished. Whoever then relaxes one of the least of these commandments and teaches men so, shall be called least in the kingdom of heaven; but he who does them and teaches them shall be called great in the kingdom of heaven" (Mt 5:17-19).

Does this mean that Jesus has nothing new to say? Obviously he does. As we have seen, his teaching about morality and law is radically new. It is summed up in what is variously called the great commandment and the new commandment of love.

St. Matthew's Gospel records an exchange between Christ and one of the scholars of the Jewish law: "A lawyer asked him a question, to test him: 'Teacher, which is the great commandment in the law?' And he said to him, 'You shall love the Lord your God with all your heart, and with all your soul, and with all your mind. This is the great and first commandment. And a second is like it, You shall love your neighbor as yourself. On these two commandments depend all the law and the prophets" (Mt 22:35-40).

And in St. John's Gospel we read: "A new commandment I give to you, that you love one another; even as I have loved you, that you also love one another. By this all men will know that you are my disciples, if you have love for one another" (Jn 13:34-35).

We commonly think of law as being concerned with justice and rights. And so it is. But Jesus tells us something else about law. For him, it is essentially a matter of love—of Christian charity. In order to express this charity in our relationships with other people, it is necessary to keep just laws, especially God's moral law taught by Jesus himself. "By this we may be sure that we know him [Jesus], if we keep his commandments. He who says 'I know him' but disobeys his commandments is a liar" (1 Jn 2:3-4).

Much more could be said about Jesus' teaching on morality and law. But what has been said at least provides the essential context for understanding the law of the Church. Ultimately, as Pope John Paul says, the Church's law is at the service of "love, grace, and charisms." Keeping that clearly in mind, we can turn now to canon law itself.

FOUR

Canon Law and the People of God

WHO ARE THE FAITHFUL? When Catholics of Holy Family Parish refer to "the faithful," they mean laypeople. That has been the expression's common meaning for a long time now, and one can hardly object to it.

Or can one? *Christifideles*, the Christian faithful, has an older and richer sense that doesn't limit its meaning only to the laity. In this broader sense, the *Christifideles* are all those who have been baptized into Christ.

This is not a quibble about words. What is at issue here touches ultimately upon one's idea of the Church and membership in her. To repeat, Christ's faithful, the *Christifideles*, are all the members of the Church: all the baptized—laity, clergy, and religious, from the pope to a tiny infant who has just been "christened." All without exception are "the faithful," and all together make up the people of God, the communion that is the Church.

The Code of Canon Law drives home this point. The second of its seven books is "The People of God," and its first part is headed "The Christian Faithful." Moreover, Title I of Part I carries the significant designation "The Obligations and Rights of All the Christian Faithful." It contains sixteen canons setting forth foundational principles regarding rights and duties common to all members of the Church. Let us see what these are.

Canon 204.1. The Christian faithful are those who, inasmuch as they have been incorporated in Christ through baptism, have been constituted as the people of God; for this reason, since they have become sharers in Christ's priestly, prophetic and royal office in their own manner, they are called to exercise the mission entrusted to the Church to fulfill in the world, in accord with the condition proper to each one.
2. This Church, constituted and organized as a society in this world, subsists in the Catholic Church, governed by the successor of Peter and the bishops in communion with him.

Article 1 of this foundational canon concisely makes the bedrock points about membership in the Church that, as we have seen, are central to the teaching of Vatican II: the fundamental equality of all in dignity and mission, arising from baptism; participation in the priestly, prophetic, and kingly ministry of Christ; shared responsibility for the Church's mission in and to the world.

The article also calls attention to the dynamic nature of Church membership. As Christians, we have work to do—the work of Christ, entrusted to and carried on by the Church. At the same time, it underlines the no less important principles of hierarchical structure and complementarity of roles and functions. The people of God is not an amorphous mass or an anarchic rabble. It is an organized, disciplined "people," with a healthy appreciation for the diversity of vocations, charisms, offices, and tasks required to accomplish the mission of restoring all things in Christ.

Where do we find this Church of Christ? Using a famous formula employed by the Council (*Lumen Gentium*, 8), Article 2 points out that it "subsists in" the Catholic Church. To be sure, as Vatican II readily added, "many elements of sanctification and of truth" exist outside the "visible structure" of the Catholic Church, in other churches and denominations; but these elements are most fully present in the Catholic Church, and indeed they possess "an inner dynamism toward Catholic unity."

Over the years there has been some confusion about exactly what it means to say Christ's Church "subsists in" the Catholic Church. In fact, it means two things: first, that Christ's Church is *inseparable* from the Catholic Church; second, that Christ's Church does not exist in the Catholic Church *exhaustively*—that is, in such a way as to exclude Christians of other traditions from also somehow belonging to it. In practical terms, the Catholics of Holy Family Parish have every reason to view and treat their Protestant neighbors as true brothers and sisters in Christ.

Canon 205. Those baptized are fully in communion with the Catholic Church on this earth who are joined with Christ in its visible structure by the bonds of profession of faith, of the sacraments, and of ecclesiastical governance.

Who belongs to the Catholic Church? Canon 205 answers: those who are united—with Christ and with the Church—by faith, sacraments, and governance.

As this and much else in canon law (as well as in Catholic doctrine) makes very clear, "the Church" is not just a spiritual entity, not some sort of mystical fellowship invisible to the naked eye. Obviously, the Catholic Church does exist as a spiritual, mystical reality. But it also is an *incarnate* Church, a human fellowship in and through Jesus Christ, with an institutional structure that is very visible indeed—for example, in a typical parish like Holy Family.

That is no accident of history and certainly not a corruption or a betrayal of God's original plan. God deals with us as we are—not disembodied spirits but flesh-and-blood human beings who are involved with one another in a variety of ways and who need visible structures in order to interact properly and be of service to one another.

The elements by which people are fully part of this communion called Church are shared faith, shared sacramental life, and acceptance of a unified system of authority governing their life in common. Already implied in the enumeration of these elements—faith, sacraments, governance—are core rights and responsibilities of members of the Church.

Canon 206.1. Catechumens are in union with the Church in a special manner, that is, under the influence of the Holy Spirit, they ask to be incorporated into the Church by explicit choice and are therefore united with the Church by that choice just as by a life of faith, hope and charity which they lead; the Church already cherishes them as its own.

2. The Church has special care for catechumens; the Church invites them to lead the evangelical life and introduces them to the celebration of sacred rites, and grants them various prerogatives which are proper to Christians.

Those who are not yet in full communion with the Church but who are consciously and deliberately on the way—catechumens—already enjoy a significant degree of unity with that which they seek. Vatican II called for the restoration of the ancient order of the adult catechumenate in its *Constitution on the Sacred Liturgy (Sacrosanctum Concilium,* 64). The Vatican published the new Rite of Christian Initiation of Adults (RCIA) in 1972.

The Introduction to the RCIA makes it clear that all members of the Church have duties not only to catechumens but to those who might become such. The first duty is the duty to evangelize: "In the various circumstances of daily life... all the followers of Christ have the obligation of spreading the faith according to their abilities."

As for those who are catechumens, the members of the local faith community, the parish, should participate in the stages of their initiation, give "honest and carefully considered testimony about them" if called upon to do so, and renew their own baptismal promises with conviction and zeal during the Easter Vigil initiation liturgy that is an annual feature of parish life in Holy Family and countless other parishes. Subsequently, Catholics offer these new members of the Church their continuing encouragement and support.

Note, though, that the RCIA is not the *only* way for adults to be received into the Catholic Church. Although the process of catechetical instruction it includes can be beneficial to many people, including Catholics themselves, it is intended particularly for adults who have not yet been baptized. Some other form of introduction to the Catholic Church may be better suited to adult Christians baptized in another denomination and now seeking to become Catholics.

Thus it would be wrong to attempt to pressure those who wish to become Catholics to participate in RCIA when they have good reasons for not doing so (age, schedule, personal temperament, for example). The community of faith has a duty to invite and *welcome* people to membership. It should not discourage them by insisting on procedures, however good in themselves, that are not obligatory but optional.

Canon 207.1. Among the Christian faithful by divine institution there exist in the Church sacred ministers, who are called clerics in law, and other Christian faithful, who are also called laity.

2. From both groups there exist Christian faithful who are consecrated to God in their own special manner and serve the salvific mission of the Church through the profession of the evangelical counsels by means of vows or other sacred bonds recognized and sanctioned by the Church. Although their state does not belong to the hierarchical structure of the Church, they nevertheless do belong to its life and holiness.

This canon about the several groups that make up the membership of the Church illustrates a striking fact about canon law in general. While its compact formulas sometimes may not seem to be saying very much, often they are saying a great deal, and sometimes as much by what they do not say as by what they do.

That is the case with Canon 207. To begin with, it lays out the hierarchical structure of the Church—clerics (deacons, priests, bishops) on the one hand, laypeople on the other—with authoritative clarity, affirming it to be God's will.

Some from both of these groups, clerics and laity, undertake a special, consecrated life as members of religious communities or secular institutes. Their way of life is not part of the Church's hierarchical structure (religious and members of secular institutes do not make up a third group, over and above clerics and laity), but it does render a service of enormous importance. Besides their service of prayer, their exemplary holiness and their many good works, they especially give witness to the "eschatological" dimension of Christian life—to the fact, that is, that final fulfillment for human beings lies not in this world but the next.

As far as the Catholic laity are concerned, however, perhaps the most important thing about this canon on the makeup of the Church is what it does not say or even imply.

There is no hint here of a top-down pyramid version of the Church in which the clergy dominate and the role of laypeople is to "pray, pay, and obey." That way of thinking is definitely not the mind of the Church. There is hierarchical structure, yes—the service of divinely commissioned leadership is indispensable and willed by God; but also a fundamental, baptismal equality in dignity as God's children and complementary roles in carrying on the Church's work.

Canons 204 through 207 are introductory. They say who the members of the Church are and, in essence, how the

Church is organized. In this way they set the stage for what follows in Canons 208 through 223: the obligations and rights which are common to all—that is, to Catholic laypeople just as much as to the clergy and religious.

Canon 208. In virtue of their rebirth in Christ there exists among all the Christian faithful a true equality with regard to dignity and in the activity whereby all cooperate in the building up of the Body of Christ in accord with each one's own condition and function.

Canon 208 is an explicit statement of a fact that we have already seen repeatedly: there is a fundamental equality, arising from baptism, among all the members of the Church with regard to their Christian dignity and their participation in the Church's mission.

But note the important qualifier at the end of the canon—"in accord with each one's own condition and function." Diversity and complementarity also are necessary within the body of Christ if the organism as a whole is to function as it should.

These principles are central to an understanding of rights and responsiblities in the Church and underlie all that follows. Here let us simply recall a key passage in Vatican II's Constitution on the Church that states the doctrinal basis of this canon:

> The chosen People of God is one: "one Lord, one faith, one baptism" (Eph 4:5). As members, they share a common dignity from their rebirth in Christ. They have the same filial grace and the same vocation to perfection... And if by the will of Christ some are made teachers, dispensers of mysteries, and shepherds on behalf of others, yet all share a true equality with regard to the dignity and to the activity common to all the faithful for the building up of the Body of Christ. Lumen Gentium, 32

Canon 209.1. The Christian faithful are bound by an obligation, even in their own patterns of activity, always to maintain communion with the Church.

2. They are to fulfill with great diligence the duties which they owe to the universal Church and to the particular church to which they belong according to the prescriptions of the law.

Canon 205 pointed out that communion with Christ and, therefore with the Church, is rooted in faith, sacraments, and governance. Canon 209 calls specific attention to the obligation of all members of the Church to *remain* in communion in all three areas.

The second article reminds us of a related matter: the obligation which all have to cultivate communion by the fulfillment of their duties toward the "universal" Church and also the "particular" church to which they belong. The meaning of "universal" Church is clear enough, but what is this "particular" church—a term not much heard in Catholic circles until fairly recently—about which the canon speaks?

For Catholics of the Latin Rite or Western Church (remember: this is the Code of Canon Law for the Western Church—the Oriental Churches or "Eastern Rites" have their own code), the answer which canon law gives is essentially this: A Catholic's particular church is his or her diocese, as determined by place of residence. The universal Church itself is a communion of these particular churches.

This does *not* mean that the Church is a kind of federation of dioceses around the world. The Catholic Church is a single, unified, organic entity. The actual relationship between the universal Church and the local Christian communities is spelled out, among other places, in a "Letter to the Bishops on the Church as Communion," published by the Congregation for the Doctrine of the Faith in 1992.

Local churches, it says, are "particular expressions of the one unique Church of Jesus Christ," and each member of the faithful belongs to the universal Church "in an *immediate* way," not by belonging to a local church. The letter calls this a "eucharistic" way of understanding the Church—for "the one-ness and indivisibility of the Eucharistic body of the Lord implies the oneness of his mystical body." Clearly, then, the communion of the local churches in and with the universal Church is not a superficial reality, a matter of organizational charts and politics.

This has special meaning in the context of American Catholicism today. One sign that all is not as it should be is the audible grumbling (even in place like Holy Family Parish and even by people who ought to know better) about alleged inter-ference by "Rome" in the affairs of something called "the American Church." As often as the Holy See steps in to disci-pline and correct—forms of service on the part of the Bishop of Rome to the Church at large that have been recognized as belonging to his office from the earliest Christian times—the "Polish Pope" and "the Curia" come in for criticism on the grounds that they "don't understand."

Although the truth of the matter often seems to be that "Rome" understands entirely too well for the complainers' comfort, it may be that the Vatican sometimes has erred, mis-read the situation in the United States, and even come down too hard on this or that. But the fact remains that this anti-Roman sentiment is a worrisome sign of slippage in the sense of membership in, and accountability to, the "universal Church," in which communion with the Bishop of Rome is an indispensable source of Catholic unity. Here is a problem that needs correcting lest it grow worse.

Canon 210. All the Christian faithful must make an effort, in accord with their own condition, to live a holy life and to pro-mote the growth of the Church and its continual sanctification.

Much has been said and written about the structural reforms and programmatic innovations initiated by Vatican II. Plainly these things are important. But the Council, in a much more important breakthrough, also recaptured for the Church an appreciation for the "universal call to holiness." The fifth chapter of the Constitution on the Church speaks of this universal call in luminous and moving terms.

Of course the Church has never lost sight of the central fact that all of its members are summoned by God to sanctity. But over the centuries, largely as a result of clericalist habits of thought among both laypeople and clergy, a kind of two-track mentality crept in. This was the minimalistic and legalistic notion that, while priests and religious indeed should aspire to sanctity, laypeople could safely be satisfied with meeting the minimum standards required to save their souls.

Vatican II, recalling the authentic Christian tradition, took a vastly different view: "All the faithful of Christ of whatever rank or status are called to the fullness of the Christian life and to the perfection of charity." Every member of the Church is called to be a saint.

Canon 210 points to the fundamental obligation arising from that fact: namely, the duty of each member of the Church to live a holy life. It also stresses that holy lives should not be understood in individualistic, me-and-God terms. Within the communion of faith, holiness has a communal dimension. Living an individual holy life requires that, to the extent he or she is able, a Catholic work for "the growth of the Church and its continual sanctification." Many canons that follow spell out how this should be done.

Canon 211. All the Christian faithful have the duty and the right to work so that the divine message of salvation may increasingly reach the whole of humankind in every age and in every land.

One assumption apparently underlying the 1917 Code of Canon Law was that evangelization was, properly speaking, a duty of the pope and the bishops. When others shared in this work, that was by way of delegation on the hierarchy's part.

Vatican II took a very different view. Having received the sacraments of baptism and confirmation, the Council teaches, every member of the Church has a right and a duty to participate in the preaching of the gospel, at least by example and, very often, by word as well.

So, for example, the Council's *Decree on the Missionary Activity of the Church* states that "the whole Church is missionary" and "the work of evangelization is a basic duty of the People of God" (*Ad Gentes*, 35). As with other elements of the Church's mission, how individuals should evangelize depends on their particular vocations, states in life, and the personal part they play, for "the lay apostolate... is a participation in the saving mission of the Church itself. Through their baptism and confirmation, all are commissioned to that apostolate by the Lord" (*Lumen Gentium*, 33).

The idea of being active evangelizers is not one that comes easily to many Catholics in Holy Family Parish. The very word "evangelization" has a Protestant sound—not to speak of the negative connotations given to it by the media, which never tire of aiming digs at "televangelists." More serious, the old idea that evangelization is the task of priests and religious, but ordinarily not of the laity persists, alongside the newer notion that, in a tolerant "ecumenical" age, all religions are equally good and God doesn't care much what church (if any) a person belongs to. This is not the place to argue at length with all these misunderstandings and confusions, but, as Canon 211 makes clear, they are *not* the Church's view.

Canon 212.1. The Christian faithful, conscious of their own responsibility, are bound by Christian obedience to follow what the sacred pastors, as representatives of Christ, declare as teachers of the faith or determine as leaders of the Church.

2. The Christian faithful are free to make known their needs, especially spiritual ones, and their desires to the pastors of the Church.

3. In accord with the knowledge, competence, and preeminence which they possess, they have the right and even at times a duty to manifest to the sacred pastors their opinion on

matters which pertain to the good of the Church, and they have a right to make their opinion known to the other Christian faithful, with due regard for the integrity of faith and morals and reverence toward their pastors, and with consideration for the common good and the dignity of persons.

This long, complex canon sets out several key principles governing the relationship between the authorities in the Church and the rest of the faithful: the duty of obedience, the right to petition the pastors regarding one's needs (which requires that the petition be heard but not that it necessarily be granted), and the right to form and express a legitimate public opinion. Without meaning to dismiss the other elements as unimportant, let us glance briefly here at this matter of "public opinion," precisely because it so often is misinterpreted.

In an age of political polls, it may not seem too surprising to find even the Code of Canon Law affirming the need for public opinion. In the Church, however, public opinion should not be understood in merely sociological or political terms. Instead, it is closely linked to "communion" itself.

A document published in 1992 by the Pontifical Council for Social Communications underlines that point. Citing what Canon 212 says about public opinion, it points out that this is partly a matter of "maintaining and enhancing the Church's credibility and effectiveness." But more fundamentally, it adds, public opinion is "one of the ways of realizing in a concrete manner the Church's character as *communio*, rooted in and mirroring the intimate communion of the Trinity. Among the members of the community who make up the Church, there is a radical equality in dignity and mission which arises from baptism and underlies hierarchical structure and diversity of office and function; and this equality necessarily will express itself in an honest and respectful sharing of information and opinions" (*Aetatis Novae*, 10).

Public opinion in the Church should be exercised on behalf of the common good by those who, as the canon points out, are qualified to do so. It assumes respect for the integrity of faith and morals. Plainly, it should not be manipulated and exploited—for example, by slanted media "leaks" intended to stir up dissent from Church teaching or foment rebellion against Church authority, as sometimes has happened in the United States and other countries in the years since Vatican II. But the right should be exercised, since healthy public opinion builds up and expresses Catholic unity. Especially it should be exercised in the context of the first principle enunciated by this canon, namely, obedience to the legitimate authority of the Church's official teachers and leaders.

Balancing the different values at stake here is a ticklish task, and conflicts have frequently occurred. Some elements of the Catholic press, for example, are accused of being bland house organs, allowing no authentic expressions of public opinion; other Catholic periodicals are viewed as intemperate, ideology-driven organs of rebellion and dissent. We shall take a closer look at some of the problems that arise under the heading of "public opinion" in a later chapter of this book. For public opinion is an obvious fact of Catholic life in the United States. Its formation and exercise go on continually in a variety of ways both appropriate and questionable.

Canon 213. The Christian faithful have the right to receive assistance from the sacred pastors out of the spiritual goods of the Church, especially the word of God and the sacraments.

This may seem an unnecessary reminder. Few if any bishops and priests, after all, are likely to refuse "the word of God and the sacraments" to Catholics who are qualified and properly disposed to receive them.

On the other hand, problems do come up. For example, in referring to the "word of God" the canon points to the duty of homilists to preach doctrinally sound homilies, and that doesn't always happen. Or again, I know of a woman on vacation who drove thirty miles on a weekday to attend First Friday

Mass at the nearest parish but arrived after Mass had ended. She asked the priest if she could at least receive Communion—and he said no: Communion outside Mass is not permitted. But it is. The same canon that discourages giving Communion indiscriminately outside Mass (918) also makes provision for it if someone requests it for a good reason. That latter provision is grounded in Canon 213.

Besides spelling out one of the fundamental rights of the faithful and pointing to one of the fundamental duties of the clergy, the canon also calls attention to a matter of great timeliness and importance today: the constant need for the hierarchy, as one writer puts it, to "organize" itself in such a way that Catholics really do have effective access to the sacraments and the word of God.

That includes relatively simple questions, such as designating the best times for Sunday Masses at Holy Family Parish—"best," among other things, from the point of view of parishioners who may have to work or travel. It also covers very complicated matters, such as how the Church can extend pastoral services to Catholics who live in remote, isolated areas or whose work or other circumstances require them to move constantly from place to place. In fact, this canon points by implication to the need for careful, comprehensive, ongoing pastoral planning at all levels—parish, diocesan, national, and even international—so that the Church can respond to the complex, fast-changing circumstances of modern life.

Canon 214. The Christian faithful have the right to worship God according to the prescriptions of their own rite approved by the legitimate pastors of the Church, and to follow their own form of spiritual life consonant with the teaching of the Church.

Diversity within the Church is not just a sociological fact but, up to a point at least, a positive, important value. This is especially true where "rites" and "spiritualities" are concerned.

Vatican II was very clear in affirming the integrity and rights of the Oriental Churches—the so-called Eastern Rites—within the Catholic Church, and devoted one of its documents specifically to them (the *Decree on Eastern Catholic Churches, Oriental - ium Ecclesiarum*).

The Code of Canon Law takes the view that people generally should remain members of the rite into which they are born, unless they have good reasons for transferring from one rite to another. Marriage to a Catholic of a different rite (see Canon 112) is such a reason.

As for diverse spiritualities, the present canon is an acknowledgment of the fact that, within the essential unity of faith, sacraments and governance among all those in full communion with the Church, there can be—and are—a variety of legitimate ways of pursuing sanctity. Typically, these correspond to the different circumstances of particular individuals and groups.

This is a matter of particular importance for Catholic laypeople. For them, the interior life is necessarily and essentially "secular" in character—it is a quest for sanctity in the midst of the world. Any form of spirituality proposed to and practiced by lay men and women must take this fundamental fact into account.

It would be impractical and wrong to try to impose a "monastic" spirituality on laypeople, who do not live their lives in monasteries but in families, offices and factories, classrooms, and a multitude of everyday secular settings. An authentic lay spirituality must recognize that for the laity work, family life, and secular activities of all kinds are the raw material of their sanctity. So, for example, the difficulties faced by a married couple in practicing Natural Family Planning out of fidelity to the Church's teaching are not so much obstacles to their holiness (as the "monastic" mentality might suppose) but means by which God wills them to become saints. (Our last chapter will go into all of this at greater length.)

Canon 215. The Christian faithful are at liberty freely to found and to govern associations for charitable and religious purposes or for the promotion of the Christian vocation in the world; they are free to hold meetings to pursue these purposes in common.

According to the pyramidal top-down vision of the Church generally taken for granted by the clericalist mentality in the past, the initiative in setting up and running religious organizations and groups—even those for the laity—came from the clerical hierarchy. Even today, many Catholics seem to assume as much.

Canon 215 rejects this way of thinking. The faithful, it says—laypeople as well as clerics and religious—have a right to set up and run religious associations on their own, without looking to the hierarchy for permission or direction. Needless to say, this doesn't mean that people can commit *the Church* as such to their private causes and interests. (On that, note the canon that follows.) It only means that Catholics as Catholics can freely associate with one another in pursuit of legitimate purposes of a broadly "religious" nature. Opus Dei, the Focolare movement, and the Charismatic Renewal are contemporary examples of Catholics doing just that. Nor is there any reason in principle why the "association" in question should not have an ecumenical dimension and involve Christians of other denominations.

Vatican II identifies three main purposes typically served by associations for lay Catholics. Such groups, it says, "sustain their members, form them for the apostolate, and rightly organize and regulate their apostolic work so that much better results can be expected than if each member were to act on his own" (*Apostolicam Actuositatem,* 18). In other words: mutual encouragement and support, spiritual, doctrinal, and perhaps even professional formation as well as coordination and collaboration for the sake of greater apostolic effectiveness.

Canon 216. All the Christian faithful, since they participate in the mission of the Church, have the right to promote or to sustain apostolic action by their own undertakings in accord with each one's state and condition; however, no undertaking shall assume the name Catholic unless the consent of competent ecclesiastical authority is given.

Group apostolic activity is an excellent thing but so is individual apostolate. Indeed, whether or not an individual joins some group apostolate, he or she has an intrinsic duty and right, grounded in baptism and confirmation, to engage in individual apostolate in one-on-one relationships. Whether or not they think of it that way, a woman who encourages her sister to return to the sacraments after many years away and a man who suggests to a co-worker with a drinking problem that he give Alcoholics Anonymous a try, are "doing apostolate." As far as laypeople are concerned, Vatican II says individual apostolate is "the origin and condition of the whole lay apostolate, even in its organized expression." And it adds that the duty to engage in activity of an apostolic nature "admits of no exception" (*Apostolicam Actuositatem*, 16).

But hierarchical structure and authority are part of the divinely willed makeup of the Church. Individuals and groups of Catholics, even if organized with apostolic ends in view, can't unilaterally commit the entire community of faith to some policy or program on their own. Decisions of that sort rest with the legitimate authorities in the Church.

Hence Canon 216's caution against claiming the name "Catholic" for private ventures undertaken by individuals and groups on their own initiative. By all means, let individual Catholics and groups of Catholics engage in apostolate without waiting to be told; but do not imply that "the Church" is answerable for the results unless those who make such decisions are willing. So, for instance, with the exception of official publications, the Catholic press is only called "Catholic" to distinguish it from the secular press. Catholic publications do not speak for the Church as such and should not be read as if they do.

Canon 217. The Christian faithful since they are called by baptism to lead a life in conformity with the teaching of the gospel, have the right to a Christian education by which they will be properly instructed so as to develop the maturity of a human person and at the same time come to know and live the mystery of salvation.

Many canons in the Code of Canon Law deal with Christian education in one way or another. From that perspective, Canon 217 is the tip of the iceberg. It is basic to much that is said elsewhere in the Code about the responsibilities and rights of the laity in general and Catholic parents in particular (as well as about the duty of the Church's pastors to provide education in the faith for the faithful, very definitely including adults).

Vatican II's *Declaration on Religious Freedom* insists that a Christian, precisely as a disciple of Christ, has a "grave obligation" to Christ himself "ever more adequately to understand the truth received from him" (*Dignitatis Humanae*, 14). It's important to note that this affirmation comes precisely in the context of the Council's teaching on religious liberty: for sometimes it is carelessly, and incorrectly, implied that what Vatican II said on this important subject offers Catholics grounds for being lax or indifferent about the faith.

Nothing could be further from the truth. Fidelity to Christ requires that Catholics study the content of their faith and, having done so, "faithfully proclaim it and vigorously defend it." All members of the Church have a grave duty to learn religious truth and participate in the work of imparting it to others.

Canon 218. Those who are engaged in the sacred disciplines enjoy a lawful freedom of inquiry and of prudently expressing their opinions on matters in which they have expertise, while observing a due respect for the magisterium of the Church.

"Sacred disciplines" refers to theology and related fields of study. The canon applies to Catholics who are involved in graduate studies in seminaries and universities. It defends their right to academic freedom (though not, it should be noted, a model of "academic freedom" simplistically borrowed from American secular academic life—where, observers of academic matters point out, the notion itself has shifted significantly in recent years, from being a safeguard for intellectual inquiry to being, in many cases, a form of job security). At the same time, the canon points to their duty to respect the Church's teaching authority—not simply for its own sake but, more fundamentally, out of concern for the common good of the community of faith.

During the last three decades few controverted issues in the Church have generated more heat than those relating to the role of theologians and to theological dissent. As part of this ongoing argument, it sometimes is suggested that the only doctrines that must be accepted are those that have been infallibly defined. This is particularly the case with elements of moral doctrine, like the teaching on abortion and contraception, where admittedly there are no formal "definitions" to guide Catholic belief. However, a strong case can be made that these things *have* been taught infallibly by the "ordinary" teaching authority of the popes and bishops.

Vatican II sheds important light on these questions in the *Constitution on the Church*. Section 25 of that document should be studied carefully by everyone who wants to know what the Church's view of this matter really is. More recently, Pope John Pau II has offered a balanced treatment in a document on Catholic universities published in 1990. There he expresses sincere appreciation for the service of theologians to the Church. But, he points out, "since theology seeks an understanding of revealed truth whose authentic interpretation is entrusted to the bishops," it is "intrinsic to the principles and methods of" theology itself that it respect the legitimate authority of the bishops and "assent to Catholic doctrine according to the degree of authority with which it is taught."

This is not a matter of knuckling under to bishops because

they can make things hot for those who defy them. The point is that in teaching the Church's authentic doctrine, bishops are performing a solemn duty of their office and rendering a vital service to the Church as a whole, and are doing so with the grace and guidance of the Holy Spirit.

Canon 219. All the Christian faithful have the right to be free from any kind of coercion in choosing a state in life.

Someone might ask: Why state the obvious? It is self-evident that nobody should be forced to adopt a particular state in life. At least by implication, however, Canon 219 calls attention to a subtler point, with undeniable relevance today.

While affirming the right to freedom from coercion in the choice of state in life, the canon does *not* affirm that anyone has a right to enter upon whatever state in life he or she happens to prefer. Is that a distinction without a difference? Hardly.

An individual's choice regarding state in life is part of his or her vocational discernment. ("Discernment" is the process by which each member of the Church should seek to determine and accept the particular role in the divine plan that God wants him or her to play.) This is not something to be done individualistically, with an eye only to personal inclination. Rather, vocational discernment must take into account the common good of the faith community. Moreover, where a particular state in life involves a public office or role in the Church's hierarchical structure, approval and validation by the authorities is a necessary part of "discernment" itself. For example, no one, on his or her own authority, can claim a "right" to be a priest (or to be a spouse, for that matter, since marriage requires the consent of another person).

In sum, then: no coercion in choosing a state of life, but no unfounded claims of "rights" either.

Canon 220. No one is permitted to damage unlawfully the good reputation which another person enjoys nor to violate

the right of another person to protect his or her own privacy.

Good name and privacy are natural human rights involving serious obligations. They are raised to a new and higher level within the Christian community by the bond of charity joining its members.

The right to a good reputation applies to groups as well as to individuals. Moreover, this right continues to be enjoyed even by those guilty of real offenses. It's not that wrongdoing may never be exposed—sometimes there may be an obligation to expose it. But someone contemplating exposing the wrongdoing of another needs to give serious thought to the question of whether and how to proceed.

In the Church especially, not every real or imagined offense needs to be made public. The Church has a hierarchical structure and a system of authority. Almost always, someone who considers someone else to be guilty of an offense should first speak privately to the suspected wrongdoer. If that fails, he or she then should call the matter to the attention of the appropriate superior of the person or persons involved, and not "go public" (at least, not until it is clear that there is no other way of dealing with an existing or threatened abuse of a serious nature).

In light of these principles, the viciousness that sometimes marks intramural conflicts among members of the Church is genuinely scandalous. Has the problem grown worse in recent years, as "liberal" and "conservative" Catholics have taken to attacking one another publicly? There are reasons to think it has. The Catholic writer and social critic Michael Novak speaks of the "visceral hatred" he's observed among Catholics engaged in assailing fellow Catholics in these ideological struggles. He is not alone in that.

Some years ago, when I was serving as press secretary to United States bishops attending a synod of bishops in Rome, I was approached by two American journalists checking out a rumor that Cardinal Joseph Ratzinger, Prefect of the Congregation for the Doctrine of the Faith (and a man much disliked by some for his vigorous defense of orthodox doctrine), was an ex-Nazi. I pointed out that, at the time World War II began, the cardinal was all of twelve years old. The journalists acted responsibly in checking, but whoever had fed them this defamatory rumor plainly did not.

Even in the setting of ordinary parishes like Holy Family, vicious flareups can and sometimes do occur. In such incidents one finds evidence of a deeply troubling phenomenon in today's Church. Unfortunately, it is not one about which canon law by itself can do very much.

Canon 221.1. The Christian faithful can legitimately vindicate and defend the rights which they enjoy in the Church before a competent ecclesiastical court in accord with the norm of law.

2. The Christian faithful also have the right, if they are summoned to judgment by competent authority, that they be judged in accord with the prescriptions of the law to be applied with equity.

3. The Christian faithful have the right not to be punished with canonical penalties except in accord with the norm of law.

This calls attention to a question that canonists and others frequently have discussed. Canon 221 speaks of a process for vindicating rights in the Church. But where, as a matter of fact, is that process to be found?

Church courts or "tribunals" deal almost exclusively with marriage cases initiated by persons seeking a formal judgment that, for one good reason or another, their "marriages" were not valid at all sacramentally. In arriving at a decision the tribunal collects and weighs evidence as any court would. During the preparation of the revised Code of Canon Law, the idea was floated to create "administrative tribunals" to handle other disputes. Nevertheless the Code in its final form says nothing specifically about them.

Still, it is not clear that this is the moment to press the issue. Canon 221 is referring to violations of authentic rights—matters of justice and injustice. In a litigious age like this, a quarrelsome period in the Church as well as in civil society, a system that appeared to invite challenges to legitimate decisions by those with the authority to make them would certainly be open to abuse. It is not far-fetched, for example, to imagine a group of disgruntled parishioners in Holy Family trying to haul their pastor before the diocesan tribunal to settle an argument over how to spend parish funds.

Canon 1419 identifies the diocesan bishop as the judge in disputes which do not belong to some other tribunal. If the bishop is a party to the dispute, however, the matter goes to the Holy See (Canon 1417). This system is not perfect, but it may be the best one here and now. Where a bishop "lives up to his title as shepherd of the diocese," remarks Father Jordan Aumann, O.P., a well-known theologian and author, the system is "still as defensible as is the judicial role of parents in a family."[1]

Not everyone agrees with that view. The last few years have seen the emergence here and there of individuals and even groups determined to use canonical procedures to vindicate the rights of Catholics who believe they have a legitimate grievance of one kind or another. One can only hope that this movement, such as it is, evolves in a healthy and positive direction.

Canon 222.1. The Christian faithful are obliged to assist with the needs of the Church so that the Church has what is necessary for divine worship, for apostolic works and works of charity, and for the decent sustenance of ministers.

2. They are also obliged to promote social justice and, mindful of the precept of the Lord, to assist the poor from their own resources.

The first article of Canon 222 underlines the duty of

Catholics to support the Church. This means financial support, of course, but not only that. Catholics should also support the programs and personnel of the Church through their personal service and involvement—"time, talent, and treasure," as a familiar formula of Christian stewardship puts it.

At the present time, the Church in the United States is experiencing serious financial problems. Dioceses throughout the country are closing institutions—Catholic schools have been major sufferers in this way—and reducing program and staff. No doubt there are many reasons, but among them is the fact that some Catholics don't give very generously to the Church—neither time nor talent nor, especially, "treasure." That the duty of stewardship, whether it takes the form of tithing or some comparably generous commitment of energies and material goods, arises from Church membership seems to have escaped the attention of numerous Catholics-in-the-pews in Holy Family and many other parishes.

This problem moved the American bishops in late 1992 to adopt a collective pastoral letter on stewardship setting out what it calls a "comprehensive view" of the obligation of Church support, rooted in Christian discipleship and vocation. "This sharing," it says, "is not an option for Catholics who understand what membership in the Church involves. It is a serious duty. It is a consequence of the faith which Catholics profess and celebrate" (National Conference of Catholic Bishops, *Stewardship: A Disciple's Response*).

The canon's second article speaks of the duty to promote social justice and help the poor. This assistance should come from the substance of our material resources, not merely the surplus. Here, however, some distinctions are needed.

Work for social justice and aid to the poor are obligations for all the faithful. But, in light of the complementarity of vocations and states in life as well as roles and functions within the Church, different groups and individuals appropriately respond to these obligations in different ways.

Thus, making allowance for possible exceptions dictated by extraordinary circumstances, it is *not* the role of the clergy to work for these good ends by engaging directly in politics, whether by holding public office or dictating specific political solutions to the laity. The main responsibility of priests and bishops in regard to the social order is to form laypeople so that they will judge clearly and act responsibly on their own initiative. The clergy do this by teaching the principles of Catholic social doctrine, whose application to concrete situations then becomes the laity's duty. For example, in the current national quest for workable welfare reform that will help people break free from dependency instead of staying mired in it, the Church's pastors appropriately identify relevant moral criteria (for example, strengthen families, don't weaken them). But it is up to laypeople to work for realistic policies and programs that embody the principles.

As for the laity, their first responsibility is to understand that they have serious obligations in conscience to work on behalf of a social order informed by justice and charity. There can be no divorce between their "religious" lives and their "secular" pursuits. Morality should shape political and economic life, work, and the professions, and the whole complex network of relationships comprising society on all levels quite as much as it should guide the private conduct of individuals.

At the same time, responsible laypeople, well formed in social doctrine, enjoy autonomy in judging and acting to bring about a social order of this kind. They should not look to the clergy for directives in these matters; doing so is an expression of the clericalist mentality at work. As Vatican II says: "Let the layman not imagine that his pastors are always such experts, that to every problem which arises, however complicated, they can readily give him a concrete solution, or even that such is their mission... Enlightened by Christian wisdom and giving close attention to the teaching authority of the Church, let the layman take on his own distinctive role" (*Gaudium et Spes*, 43).

Canon 223.1. In exercising their rights the Christian faithful, both as individuals and when gathered in associations, must take account of the common good of the Church and of the rights of others as well as their own duties toward others.

2. In the interest of the common good, ecclesiastical authority has competence to regulate the exercise of the rights which belong to the Christian faithful.

The rights and responsibilities of Catholics as members of the Church are not grounded in an individualistic view of what it means to be one of the *Christifideles*, part of the people of God. As we have seen, the ecclesiology underlying the Code of Canon Law is a vision of the Church as a communion, a "body," where complementarity of function and a hierarchical structure involving authority and accountability both are crucial.

In calling attention to these matters, Canon 223 cites the common good of the Church, the rights of others, and the role of legitimate authority as key principles guiding and governing the exercise of rights and the fulfillment of duties on the part of individual Catholics and groups of Catholics.

The Second Vatican Council, as we also have seen, defines the common good as the sum total of those conditions of social life by which "individuals, families, and groups can achieve their own fulfillment in a relatively thorough and ready way." Although this refers to the "common good" of civil secular society, the common good of the Church, while assuming the same material and temporal needs on the part of its members, looks beyond them, understanding "fulfillment" in its ultimate, integral sense: perfect fulfillment in and through Christ in respect to all the goods of the human person—most completely, the fulfillment of eternal life in heaven.

It follows, then, that the exercise of rights and the fulfillment of responsibilities by the *Christifideles* must take the temporal needs and interests of others into account. But the ultimate norm and objective of Christian duties and rights concern that final fulfillment of which Vatican II speaks. The Church, it says, will reach "her full perfection only in the glory of heaven." Meanwhile, "we perform, with hope of good things to come, the task committed to us in this world by the Father."

FIVE

Obligations and Rights of the Laity

A FTER TREATING (IN TITLE I) the rights and responsibilities common to *all* members of the Church, including laypeople, Book II of the Code of Canon Law turns (in Title II, "The Obligations and Rights of the Lay Christian Faithful") to those that concern the laity in particular.

The 1917 Code contained two canons dealing specifically with lay rights. One affirmed that laypeople are entitled to receive the sacraments; the other said the laity may not wear ecclesiastical garb. The present section of the 1983 Code contains eight canons. That raises a question: Does a net gain of six canons in Church law measure the progress of the Catholic laity from 1917 to 1983?

The answer of course is no, even where canon law is concerned. What the Code says about the responsibilities and rights of laypeople is not limited to this relatively short section.

The remainder of the 1983 Code contains numerous canons pertaining to the laity—often, along with clerics and religious—in a variety of contexts.

Title II's eight canons nevertheless are extremely important. They are the foundation, the basis, for much else. They identify basic duties and rights underlying specific obligations and entitlements treated elsewhere in the law. For this reason they deserve close study and reflection in their own right.

WHO ARE THE LAITY?

But before we look at these canons, there's a prior question to consider: Who are the laity? To be sure, that is not something most people in Holy Family Parish spend a lot of time fretting about. Still, there are some real issues at stake here—issues more complicated than may at first be apparent.

The old answer was simple, straightforward—and off-putting: laypeople are members of the Church who are not clerics (or, neither clerics nor religious). That is technically correct but alienating and negative. As a definition, it does not encourage laypeople to take a very exalted view of their Christian dignity or to involve themselves very deeply in the mission of their Church. It easily lends itself to the pray-pay-and-obey view of the laity.

"The Synod Fathers have rightly pointed to the need for a definition of the lay faithful's vocation and mission in *positive terms*." That is Pope John Paul II speaking, in his 1989 document "The Lay Members of Christ's Faithful People." Citing Vatican Council II, the 1987 Synod of Bishops on the Laity, other recent doctrinal statements, and "the lived experience of the Church, guided as she is by the Holy Spirit," the Pope describes the laity in dynamic terms placing them at the center of the Church's mission rather than far off on the passive fringe.

The essence of this new understanding of Catholic lay-people, as we have already seen, lies in this: "Through Baptism the lay faithful are made one body with Christ and are established among the People of God. They are in their own way made sharers in the priestly, prophetic and kingly office of Christ."

In their own way... A good definition calls attention to what is special about what it defines. What is special about the laity—what distinguishes them from priests and religious? Echoing Vatican II, Pope John Paul says it is their "secular character." He explains what that means in an important passage that deserves to be quoted at length:

The "world" thus becomes the place and the means for the lay faithful to fulfill their Christian vocation because the world itself is destined to glorify God the Father in Christ.... They are not called to abandon the position that they have in the world. Baptism does not take them from the world at all.... On the contrary, God entrusts a vocation to them that properly concerns their situation in the world.

The lay faithful, in fact, "are called by God so that they, led by the spirit of the Gospel, might contribute to the sanctification of the world, as from within like leaven, by fulfilling their own particular duties. Thus, especially in this way of life, resplendent in faith, hope and charity they manifest Christ to others." Lumen Gentium, 31

Thus for the lay faithful, to be present and active in the world is not only an anthropological and sociological reality, but in a specific way, a theological and ecclesiological reality as well. In fact, in their situation in the world, God manifests his plan and communicates to them their particular vocation of "seeking the Kingdom of God by engaging in temporal affairs and by ordering them according to the plan of God." Christifidelis Laici, 15

The secular character of the Catholic laity—the fact that

they live and work in the world—is not something separate from, much less opposed to, their identity as members of the Church. Rather, it's part of their Christian identity, an essential element in their vocation as laypeople, that sets them apart from the *Christifideles* who are clergy and religious. The lay vocation—the vocation entrusted to them by God—is a vocation in and to the secular world. The laity's role in the mission of the Church is to work for the world's redemption. This is not a second-rate calling for second-rate Christians, and it is a far cry from "pray, pay, and obey." It is central to what the Church is all about.

This understanding of the Catholic laity is, then, essential to an accurate understanding of what canon law says about "The Obligations and Rights of the Lay Christian Faithful."

Canon 224. In addition to those obligations and rights which are common to all the Christian faithful and those which are determined in other canons, the lay Christian faithful are bound by the obligations and possess the rights which are enumerated in the canons of this title.

Good law is precise. In order to prevent any confusion and allay any anxiety, Canon 224 underlines the obvious: the rights and responsibilities of laypeople include not only those set out in the canons that immediately follow in this section but also those noted immediately above as "common to all," as well as various fundamental duties and rights prescribed elsewhere in the Code (for example, on the subject of parents' rights).

In general terms, these rights and obligations concern education and spiritual formation, participation in the sacramental life of the Church, participation in apostolate and in ministries, and sharing in ecclesiastical governance and decision-making. We shall be looking at many of these functions as we work our way through the canons which follow.

Canon 225.1. Since the laity, like all the Christian faithful,

are deputed by God to the apostolate through their baptism and confirmation, they are therefore bound by the general obligations and enjoy the general right to work as individuals or in associations so that the divine message of salvation becomes known and accepted by all persons throughout the world; this obligation has a greater impelling force in those circumstances in which people can hear the gospel and know Christ only through lay persons.

2. Each lay person in accord with his or her condition is bound by a special duty to imbue and perfect the order of temporal affairs with the spirit of the gospel; they thus give witness to Christ in a special way in carrying out those affairs and in exercising secular duties.

Evangelization is the generic name for the activity with which this canon is concerned. In general terms, evangelization—spreading the Good News of Jesus Christ—is the mission of the Church.

Vatican II points out that evangelization is basic, essential, to everything else the Church does. By the proclamation of the gospel, the *Constitution on the Church* says, she "prepares her hearers to receive and profess the faith, disposes them for baptism, snatches them from the slavery of error, and incorporates them into Christ so that through charity they may grow up into full maturity in Christ."

Catholic evangelizers have been announcing the Good News from time immemorial. Specifically missionary work has an ancient and honorable history, as the Acts of the Apostles attests. For a long time, however, not only were the "missionaries" almost exclusively priests and religious—it was generally taken for granted that that was how things ought to be.

Today this is no longer so. The Council clearly and firmly situates laypeople at the heart of evangelization. "The obligation of spreading the faith is imposed on every disciple of Christ," the *Constitution on the Church* declares. The right and duty to evangelize are not a concession to the laity or a task assigned by bishops and priests inviting them to lend a hand. The laity have a duty and a right to evangelize simply because they are members of the Church. That message has been repeated time and again by popes and bishops. Canon 225 makes it part of canon law.

The canon also does several other things.

It spells out that the laity have a right to engage in evangelization either as individuals or in associations formed for this purpose. It notes that, in the contemporary circumstances of a highly secularized culture, it frequently is the case that Catholic evangelization either will be done by laypeople or not at all. Laity can and will fulfill their obligation in this regard in a multitude of different ways, according to their temperaments and talents, their situations and opportunities. But the canon further points out that a lay person's contribution to evangelization especially involves infusing gospel values into the structures and institutions of secular society—a form of activity that, as Pope John Paul observes, echoing Vatican II, is the specific vocation proper to laypeople.

Generally speaking, evangelizing activity falls into two broad categories. Part of it is what is traditionally called "missionary" work—preaching the gospel in places where it has not been preached before and people have had little or no exposure to the message of Jesus Christ. Against false ideas regarding religious tolerance and ecumenism, Pope John Paul ringingly affirmed the continued need for this form of activity in an encyclical called *The Mission of the Redeemer* (1991) that also recognizes the role of the laity in mission work.

The other form of evangelization involves bringing the gospel to people nearby—neighbors, friends, family members, fellow workers—who need to learn of Jesus and his message. It goes without saying that this is something laypeople can and should do, and that it almost certainly will not get done otherwise.

Part of it is good example—the witness of life, lived as a Christian—and part of it, as circumstances permit, requires speaking up in explanation and defense of Christian truth. In recent years, too, Pope John Paul has given particular emphasis to what he often calls "re-evangelization": a renewed proclamation of Christ and his good news to formerly Christian but now heavily secularized (even paganized) societies of the West, where practicing Christians have become a (sometimes small) minority.

How well is this vision being realized today? Certainly there are dedicated laypeople who take their right and responsibility to evangelize very seriously. There are even Catholic "lay missionaries" who commit themselves to this work, at home or abroad, for a period of time.

Still, many laypeople do not seem very aware that they have a duty and a right to evangelize by the witness of life, and, consciously at least, many do not do very much about it. Apparently, the attitude that "missionary work" is the responsibility of priests and nuns is still widespread. This is a serious obstacle to effective evangelization. We shall see more about it later in this book.

Canon 226.1. Lay persons who live in the married state in accord with their own vocation are bound by a special duty to work for the upbuilding of the people of God through their marriage and their family.

2. Because they have given life to their children, parents have a most serious obligation and enjoy the right to educate them; therefore, Christian parents are especially to care for the Christian education of their children according to the teaching handed on by the Church.

The 1983 Code of Canon Law has a great deal to say about marriage, family life, and the roles of spouses and parents, especially in regard to the education and formation of their children. As one canonist remarks, Canon 226 provides the basis for "a veritable bill of parental rights and obligations" identified in various places in the Code.

In this, it mirrors Vatican II, which affirms that marriage is a vocation. It calls marriage and family life a path to sanctity and repeats the Church's teaching that parents are the primary educators of their children—a fact that carries with it important rights to be respected by authorities in Church and state alike, along with serious obligations in whose fulfillment parents have a right to look to Church and state for help. These matters will be discussed at greater length below.

Here, though, it's important to unravel what might appear to be a mystery.

In speaking of the "special duty" that married people are said to have for the "upbuilding of the people of God," isn't Canon 226 being hopelessly unrealistic and even unfair? Most married couples, especially those with children, have their hands full as it is. That is certainly how it is for young couples with youngsters in Holy Family Parish. The canon appears to be piling yet another obligation—Church work of some unspecified kind—upon people who in many cases are already overburdened.

But this sort of piling-on of obligations is unjust to those who are conscientious, and it also gives rise to the cynicism that customarily greets laws that make unreasonable demands. Is Canon 226 talking through its hat? Can it—might one even say, should it—be ignored?

Before being too quick to answer yes, we need to look again at what the canon actually says. It does not tell married people to take on a heavy agenda of Church-related activities *outside* the home. Instead, it calls attention to their obligation to build up the people of God precisely *through* their marriage and family life. That happens mainly within the home, not outside it.

The Constitution on the Church, in a phrase used many times in Catholic documents since then, speaks of the Christian family as a "domestic Church." That is a very rich way of thinking of the family; it deserves prayerful consideration by family members.

Vatican II sketches out the basic ideas this way: "From the wedlock of Christians there comes the family, in which new citizens of human society are born. By the grace of the Holy Spirit received in baptism these are made children of God, thus perpetuating the People of God through the centuries. The family is, so to speak, the domestic Church. In it parents should, by their word and example, be the first preachers of the faith to their children" (*Lumen Gentium*, 11). That is a high calling indeed; it demands the best energies of spouses and parents.

The second article of Canon 226 specifically underlines the educational task of parents, implied in article one, with particular attention to the religious formation of children. In line with the Church's traditional view of marriage and family life, it affirms the primacy of parents in educational matters. Not only chronologically but as a matter of right and duty, parents are the first educators of their children. Their role as educators is "so decisive," says Vatican II in its *Declaration on Christian Education*, "that scarcely anything can compensate for their failure in it" (*Gravissimum Educationis*, 3). We shall consider this matter, as well as other questions pertaining to marriage and family life, at greater length below.

Canon 227. Lay Christian faithful have the right to have recognized that freedom in the affairs of the earthly city which belongs to all citizens; when they exercise such freedom, however, they are to take care that their actions are imbued with the spirit of the gospel and take into account the doctrine set forth by the magisterium of the Church; but they are to avoid proposing their own opinion as the teaching of the Church in questions which are open to various opinions.

It is an ancient canard sometimes aimed at lay Catholics participating in public life and carrying out the duties of citizenship that they are under the thumb of the hierarchy, required to do the bidding of bishops and priests. Even today, in the democratic, tolerant United States, this anti-Catholic slur now and then is repeated by people who ought to know better. Canon 227 gives the lie to such claims: The Catholic laity, it says, enjoy the same freedom in secular affairs as everybody else.

But authentic freedom is not subjective license. Freedom carries with it an obligation that it be used properly. There is an objective order of moral truth: the natural law and, beyond it, other principles of morality that are made known by divine revelation. The Church's magisterium teaches moral principles and norms with authority. In forming their consciences, Catholics should be guided by this teaching—without, however, supposing that the representatives of the magisterium either can or should supply answers to each and every concrete question pertaining to the conduct of secular affairs.

Finally, the canon cautions laypeople against presenting their opinions as the "Catholic" solutions to social problems. This is not a farfetched warning, as any regular reader of conservative and liberal Catholic periodicals knows all too well.

Some social policies and programs plainly are *not* compatible with moral truth, and these should be rejected, by Catholics as by everybody else. For example, legal abortion and euthanasia are no more acceptable today than, say, slavery and racial segregation were in times gone by, when first one and then the other were legal and widely approved. However, political and social problems often are complex, the right solutions often are unclear, and not infrequently there is more than one solution that is—or, to reasonable people, at least seems to be—both workable and morally acceptable.

The United States bishops' 1983 collective pastoral letter on war and peace referred to this reality. "On some complex social questions," it remarked, "the Church expects a certain diversity of views even though all hold the same universal moral principles." In such circumstances, Catholics of differing political and ideological persuasions should grant one another the right to argue and work for the solutions they think best, without attempting to use "the Church" or "social doctrine" as a club against those who disagree with them.

Canon 228.1. Qualified lay persons are capable of assuming from their sacred pastors those ecclesiastical offices and functions which they are able to exercise in accord with the prescriptions of law.

2. Lay persons who excel in the necessary knowledge, prudence, and uprightness are capable of assisting the pastors of the Church as experts or advisors; they can do so even in councils, in accord with the norm of law.

We are light years removed here from a situation in which holy orders is a prerequisite for holding any office in the Church. Canon 228 admits laypeople to ecclesiastical decision-making and governing bodies, as well as to advisory functions. Other canons, in various places throughout the Code, identify particular offices they can hold or else make it clear that this is something for local authority to decide (for example, Canon 469, which concerns the "diocesan curia"—the administrative structure of a diocese).

The canon says laypeople who hold ecclesiastical office or serve as advisors must be qualified—they must possess knowledge, prudence, and uprightness. So of course must anyone else, cleric or religious, who occupies an ecclesiastical office or functions as an "expert" of one kind or another. Specialized work naturally requires particular training, but the basic qualifications for performing in a consultative role are good sense and relevant experience. These are possessed by lay men and women just as much as they are by anyone else.

That said, however, a cautionary note is necessary. Making due allowance for the variety of individual vocations as well as for diverse local conditions and needs, most laypeople not only will not but also should not look to the Church for their professional careers.

As we have already seen, the apostolate proper to the laity lies in and to the secular world, including the world of everyday work. This essential point is in danger of being obscured when a spirit of clericalist elitism leads large numbers of laypeople to seek jobs in the ecclesiastical bureaucracy, in the belief that this is a "higher" calling than the calling to bring Christian values to bear upon secular professions and jobs.

However, laypeople in large numbers also can and should lend their expertise to the Church by serving as advisors and participating in consultative bodies at all levels. Parish and diocesan pastoral councils are expressions of this, as are similar entities at the national (as part of the structure of the National Conference of Catholic Bishops and the United States Catholic Conference) and even at the international level (where laypeople serve as advisers to numerous bodies of the Holy See). As one author remarks: "The function of counselling is based on the virtue of prudence... and on the personal expertise of the counsellor; and neither of these properties is exclusive to clerics or religious, for both virtue and art come, not from holy orders or religious profession, but from study, experience and *sensus Ecclesiae*, all of which are common to clerics, religious and laity alike."[1]

Canon 229.1. Lay persons are bound by the obligation and possess the right to acquire a knowledge of Christian doctrine adapted to their capacity and condition so that they can live in accord with that doctrine, announce it, defend it when necessary, and be enabled to assume their role in exercising the apostolate.

2. Lay persons also possess the right to acquire that deeper knowledge of the sacred sciences which are taught in ecclesiastical universities or faculties or in institutes of religious sciences by attending classes and obtaining academic degrees.

3. Likewise, the prescriptions as to the required suitability having been observed, lay persons are capable of receiving from legitimate ecclesiastical authority a mandate to teach the sacred sciences.

In recent years, laypeople in small but growing numbers have emerged as students or professors of theology and other ecclesiastical disciplines in seminaries and similar Church-related institutions. The second and third articles of Canon 229 extend formal recognition to this trend and reject unfairly discriminatory attitudes and practices of the past, when the advanced study and teaching of theology in effect were limited to priests and candidates for the priesthood.

For most laypeople, however, it is article one that really matters. Most important, perhaps, is what it says about the obligation of lay men and women to acquire a solid knowledge of the faith as a necessary basis for their apostolate in the world.

No doubt it is desirable to have a corps of well-trained lay professors of theology in seminaries and advanced theological institutes. But it is even more important that Catholic workers and professional people of all kinds—doctors, bankers, sales-persons, teachers, farmers, military officers, computer opera-tors, mechanics, and the rest—know Catholic doctrine and be able to explain it and defend it to others.

The tragedy is that far fewer Catholics are able to do this than should be. Ignorance of their faith makes such people easy game for groups and movements—from fundamentalists to secular humanists—who have no sympathy for the Church. And obviously such ignorance ill equips them to proclaim the gospel, to evangelize.

The remedy for this situation does not lie in offering lay-people elementary catechesis, a kind of intellectual pabulum for adults (although remedial instruction may be required in cases where religious education has been severely neglected for a long period of time). The remedy is "solid doctrinal instruc-tion in theology, ethics, and philosophy... adjusted to differ-ences of age, status, and natural talents" of which Vatican II speaks in its *Decree on the Apostolate of the Laity*. Some Church-related programs and institutions labor valiantly to meet this need. One that comes to mind is the Catholic Home Study Institute of Leesburg, Virginia, which offers well-prepared, doctrinally sound correspondence courses in the faith of the

Church. Some parishes also have successful programs. In Holy Family, like many other places, though, "adult education" is a catch-as-catch-can, now-and-then kind of thing that the associate pastor, Father Ross, struggles to keep going without much support.

Canon 230.1. Lay men who possess the age and qualifications determined by decree of the conference of bishops can be installed on a stable basis in the ministries of lector and acolyte in accord with the prescribed liturgical rite; the conferral of these ministries, however, does not confer on these lay men a right to obtain support or remuneration from the Church.

2. Lay persons can fulfill the function of lector during liturgical actions by temporary deputation; likewise all lay persons can fulfill the functions of commentator or cantor or other functions, in accord with the norm of law.

3. When the necessity of the Church warrants it and when ministers are lacking, lay persons, even if they are not lectors or acolytes, can also supply for certain of their offices, namely, to exercise the ministry of the word, to preside over liturgical prayers, to confer baptism, and to distribute Holy Communion in accord with the prescriptions of the law.

This canon repeats the essence of a document issued by Pope Paul VI in 1972 (*Ministeria Quaedam*) that did away with the former "minor orders" (porter, lector, exorcist, and acolyte) as well as tonsure and the subdiaconate, and expanded the opportunities for laypeople to perform liturgical roles or "ministries." These were innovative steps for Pope Paul VI to take, yet by any realistic standard they concerned matters of less than central importance in the life of the Church.

Even so, Canon 230 has been the focal point of a great deal of heated controversy in some Catholic circles. That is probably unavoidable, but it also is unfortunate, for the controversy has less to do with the subject matter of the canon itself than with other issues now dividing Catholics.

The first article says lay men—men only, that is—can be "installed" in the permanent ministries of lector and acolyte. The second article says lay women as well as men can nevertheless serve on a temporary basis as lectors, cantors, and in other liturgical functions, without being installed in the ministries. The third article says that in the absence of ministers, other lay people, men and women, can do several of the things lectors and acolytes do—preside over liturgical prayers, confer baptism, distribute Holy Communion—as the need of the Church dictates.

Inevitably, the canon has become embroiled in the ongoing controversy over the role of women in the Church. For one thing, it restricts the permanent ministries of lector and acolyte to men. For another, it rules out female altar servers (or at least it seems to do that: some people think otherwise). But it also allows women (along with men) to perform a number of functions in the liturgy that most people would say are a lot more important than "serving Mass." Does all this make much sense?

A second controversy swirls specifically around article three, which assigns to laypeople several liturgical functions (leading prayers, baptizing, distributing Communion) on the basis of the "necessity of the Church." Obviously, though, in many typical parishes like Holy Family, laypeople routinely do at least some of these things, especially distributing Communion, not because there aren't enough priests or deacons or potential candidates for the "installed" ministries, but simply because the laity are regularly assigned to do them.

But should that be the case? Possibly. Still, not everyone agrees. In fact, some people see a looming danger in the proliferation of lay liturgical roles: the clericalization of the laity—a tacit acceptance of the notion that truly committed, exemplary laypeople are those who most resemble priests, along with a tacit de-emphasis of the ideal of lay apostolate in and to the secular world.

Noting such problems, controversies and confusions as these, all centering on the interpretation of *Ministeria Quaedam* (and so, of course, on Canon 230), Pope John Paul in his 1989 apostolic constitution on the laity announced the establishment of a papal commission "to provide an in-depth study of the various theological, liturgical, juridical, and pastoral considerations which are associated with the great increase today of the ministries entrusted to the lay faithful." And, as this is written, the Vatican recently has indicated that some resolution of these matters may soon be forthcoming. It is desirable that it should.

Canon 231.1. Lay persons who devote themselves permanently or temporarily to some special service of the Church are obliged to acquire the appropriate formation which is required to fulfill their function properly and to carry it out conscientiously, zealously, and diligently.

2. With due regard for can. 230.1, they have a right to decent remuneration suited to their condition; by such remuneration they should also be able to provide decently for their own needs and for those of their family with due regard for the prescriptions of civil law; they likewise have a right that their pension, social security, and health benefits be duly provided.

Church law states principles of justice. It does not explain how to put them into effect or how to reconcile them with other values with which they are, or may be, in tension. That can be frustrating.

Canon 231.2 is an example. Who today would seriously doubt that laypeople who work for the Church ought to get fair salaries and fringe benefits? No doubt what is "fair" depends on particular circumstances and situations, and sincere people of good will can disagree about what is fair in a given case. Still, fairness in remuneration is the norm. Church institutions have no right to shave costs by underpaying lay employees.

True enough. But this universally accepted principle also raises certain difficulties.

As everyone is aware, the number of lay staff has risen sharply in Church-related institutions like schools and hospitals in recent years as the number of religious and priests has declined. (In Holy Family School, only the principal and the second-grade teacher are nuns.) And, while this has been happening, the cost of running these institutions also has risen steeply. One reason, though certainly not the only one, is that lay staff are more expensive than clerics and religious.

As the cost of Church-related institutions goes up, however, they naturally tend to be patronized by those who can afford to pay. In the absence of subsidization—by the Church, government, or the private sector—those who can't pay must go elsewhere. The longterm implications are disturbing. In the worst-case scenario, the Church ends up running schools and other institutions and programs only for the benefit of those who are relatively well-off—an outcome neither desirable nor even acceptable from the Church's point of view. If there is an easy solution to this problem, no one has yet said what it is.

Again: candor requires recognition of a certain tension between the principle of fair pay for lay employees and the spirit of generous, self-sacrificing service that ideally ought to motivate those who staff the Church's institutions and programs.

Granted, there is no absolute conflict here. Fairly paid lay teachers or hospital workers can indeed be—and often are—highly dedicated individuals who approach their work in an apostolic spirit. But inevitably the situation does involve a kind of built-in invitation to careerism. Working in the programs and institutions of the Church, once thought of in terms of vocation, is at risk of becoming only a job. That is not an argument against paying laypeople fairly. It is an argument for giving particular emphasis to the apostolic dimension of Church work, along with providing fair pay and benefits.

Perhaps that dovetails with article one of Canon 230 and its stress on "formation" for the lay men and women who work for the Church. While the canon underlines the obligation that such people have to seek formation, it is fair also to point out that Church-related programs and institutions have a duty to provide it. Some do. But, as a layman who has spent the better part of four decades working professionally for a succession of Church organizations, I must report that even now many do not. That is a troubling omission.

So much for Titles I and II of Part I of "The People of God." They lay out the basic canonical principles concerning the rights and duties of the laity as members of Church. (Title III goes on to deal with "Sacred Ministers or Clerics," while almost all of the third and last part of "The People of God" concerns religious.)

As abstract statements of obligation and right, these canons pertaining to Catholic laypeople are for the most part admirably clear. But, as everyone realizes, it often is a lot easier to make abstract statements about how things ought to be than it is to translate them into concrete reality. These sections of the revised Code of Canon Law reflect enormous progress in the Church's thinking about the laity. But the principles they express must be applied, and unresolved questions and problems must be recognized and addressed.

In the chapters that follow, we shall be doing some of both—applying principles and examining problems that hinder the exercise of rights and the fulfillment of responsibilities on the part of Catholic laypeople today. This is *not*, to repeat, an exercise in the technical interpretation and application of canon law, for that is something best left to specialists. The idea instead is to explore what these fundamental principles mean in practical terms in the ordinary life of the Church and its members. We shall start with a basic source of much misunderstanding: confusion and conflict over the meaning of "power" in the Church.

SIX

Rights versus Responsibilities?

WHO'S RUNNING THE SHOW at Holy Family and parishes like it, the pastor or the parishioners? Who ought to be? Is life in the Church a perpetual power struggle? Is that what Church membership really means?

Put it that way, of course, and not many people are likely to endorse the idea of power struggle in the Church. And yet... doesn't it sometimes look as if something like a political "power struggle" were the model of Christian life as some contemporary Catholics see it?

Clergy versus laity. Priests versus bishops. Liberals versus conservatives. Women versus men. Affluent suburban parishes versus poor inner city ones. This racial or ethnic group versus that one. The "American Church" versus "Rome." These days relationships between and among different groups of Catholics are often framed in just such terms: somebody or something *versus* somebody or something else. That is the great danger—and the truly perverse ("twisted") outcome—of taking a false view of rights and responsibilities in the Church.

The various theologies of "liberation" tend to encourage this result on principle. Borrowed originally from Marxism, the liberationist mode of analysis understands history itself in terms of a "dialectical" process—thesis, antithesis, and synthesis—repeated over and over until some final consummation, whether that be in or out of time. The driving force of this process shaping history is the struggle of the oppressed against their oppressors.

Classical Marxists, viewing history in terms of class struggle (the poor against the rich, the proletariat against the capitalists), interpret the ebb and flow of forces in secular society in its light. Communism may now be dead, but the Marxist notion that this is the underlying pattern working itself out in a multitude of social contexts remains alive and well.

It is found, for instance, among Christian liberationists, whose particular focus is the Church. Hence the appeals heard in recent years (especially in Latin America) for the creation of a "People's Church." Hence, too, the angry denunciations (common today in U.S. Catholic circles influenced by secular feminism) of "hierarchical" and "patriarchal" domination.

The liberationists have a point, of course. These are complex matters. There is no denying the historical fact of abuses of power and authority in the Church, nor can one realistically deny that their effects, both recognized and unrecognized, linger on today. Ecclesiastical structures and institutions, to the extent that they are human inventions created and conducted by imperfect human beings, could always be better than they are. So, naturally, could the human members of the Church.

Yet relationships within the Christian community are not ultimately reducible in principle to a power struggle. Someone who thinks of Christian life in those terms is not thinking of "Christian life" at all. Nor can the entity he or she has in mind realistically be described as a "community." It is questionable whether, or in what sense, it can be called "the Church."

The problem, one might say, was anticipated very early. "I fear that perhaps I may come and find you not what I wish... that perhaps there may be quarrelling, jealousy, anger, selfishness, slander, gossip, conceit, and disorder." Thus St. Paul addressed the fractious Christians of Corinth—apparently not without reason (2 Cor 12:20). Earlier, in a memorable image, he had underlined the destructive absurdity of such behavior among those who claim to be, collectively, the body of Christ:

> If the foot should say, "Because I am not a hand, I do not belong to the body," that would not make it any less a part of the body. And if the ear should say, "Because I am not an eye, I do not belong to the body," that would not make it any less a part of the body. If the whole body were an eye, where would be the hearing? If the whole body were an ear, where would be the sense of smell? But as it is, God arranged the organs in the body, each one of them, as he chose.... There are many parts, yet one body.... Now you are the body of Christ. 1 Cor 12:15-20, 27.

Catholic laypeople need to take all this very seriously as they reach out—quite properly—to claim their rights and exercise their responsibilities in the Church. What is this great, ongoing lay movement in contemporary Catholicism all about? A power struggle?

According to Cormac Burke, "'power-sharing' has become a sort of slogan in certain ecclesiastical quarters to describe what is considered to be an essential condition for renewal." At its most extreme, he says, this way of thinking about the "advancement of the laity" signifies "promotion into the power-echelons within the Church, so that the laity can at last recover the power which was wrongfully taken from them. The laity will then no longer be under the domination of the hierarchy."[1] Then, no doubt, he adds, we shall have a genuine people's Church.

There are those who consider such goals worth fighting for, but they are irreducibly, tragically wrong. For if the whole body were an eye, where would be the hearing? If the whole body were an ear, where would be the sense of smell? If life in the Church is simply a scramble for status and power, what becomes of the body of Christ? *This* is not where our rights and responsibilities as Catholics should carry us.

Where then? The answer, repeated time and again during and since the Second Vatican Council, is this: Authority in the Church is essentially a mode of service; power itself is a capacity to serve.

Jesus taught that lesson, in deeds and words, when he washed his apostles' feet at the Last Supper: "Do you know what I have done to you? You call me Teacher and Lord; and you are right, for so I am. If I then, your Lord and Teacher, have washed your feet, you also ought to wash one another's feet. For I have given you an example, that you also should do as I have done to you" (Jn 13:12-15).

Vatican II, speaking of the hierarchical structure willed for the Church by Christ, sums it up this way: "For the nurturing and constant growth of the People of God, Christ the Lord instituted in His Church a variety of ministries, which work for the good of the whole body. For those ministers who are endowed with sacred power are servants of their brethren, so that all who are of the People of God, and therefore enjoy a true Christian dignity, can work toward a common goal freely and in an orderly way, and arrive at salvation" (*Lumen Gentium*, 18).

Against this background, it is clear, whether we are talking about Holy Family Parish or the Church Universal, that a healthy approach to rights and responsibilities must aim at enhancing the effectiveness of all the Church's members in rendering service. That requires a clear, accurate understanding of rights and responsibilities themselves.

A PRIMER OF RIGHTS AND RESPONSIBILITIES

What are these things called rights and responsibilities? The answer is not as obvious as it may seem at first. A great deal is said these days about rights and responsibilities—about rights especially—but a lot that is said is based on shaky assumptions.

Perhaps the shakiest of these, as well as the one with the deepest roots in our less than perfect human nature, is the idea that rights and responsibilities are necessarily, inescapably in tension, if not indeed in outright conflict. In fact, that kind of thinking easily can turn out to be a self-fulfilling prophecy. Rights and responsibilities very likely will clash with one another in the lives of individuals who think of them that way.

It comes easy to such people to claim as many rights and shirk as many responsibilities as they possibly can (that is called "looking out for number one"). When this pattern of behavior brings them into conflict with others, as sooner or later it will, then so much the worse for the others.

The truth of the matter is profoundly different. "Right and duty are the same reality," says the distinguished Catholic moral theologian Germain Grisez. Right and responsibility are not opposed to each other; they are different aspects of the same thing. Indeed, there are no authentic rights apart from duties that correspond to them.

That is far from clear in a lot of contemporary "rights talk," where rights are claimed and defended as if they were independent, self-evident moral principles standing on their own and needing justification from no other source.

Obviously, as another Catholic moral thinker, John Finnis of Oxford University, remarks, the idea of rights does have "its appropriateness and its power." That is because it contains, at bottom, the two ideas of individuality and equality: each of us is unique; all of us are essentially equal.

But not all rights talk is like that. On the contrary, as Finnis points out, "We are surrounded and sometimes deafened by claims of right in which the very reference to rights seems somehow wrong." He cites as examples the claims not infrequently made to such things as the "right to success," the "right to good health," the "right to a rising standard of living" and, most especially, the right, asserted and obstinately defended by the United States Supreme Court, to kill the unborn by abortion.

"In all these and countless other uses of the word 'rights' or 'human rights,'" Finnis says, "we can, if we listen, hear another aspect, another resonance: not the unique and thus equal status of each and every human being, but *my* status, *my* interest.... So the language of rights is supremely suited to expressing, persuasively, the egoism by which I treat other people's interests as mere matters of convenience, to be overridden by or subordinated and redirected to favor *my* interests."[2]

Evidently it's imperative to do some careful sorting-out lest we talk too quickly and casually about rights and responsibilities—in particular, about our rights and *somebody else's* responsibilities.

A good place to begin is by distinguishing different kinds of rights. John Finnis identifies three: First, the right to do things and also *not* to do things. Nothing very complicated about that. One has a right, for instance, to know the truth and to worship God; and also a right not to take falsehoods for truth or engage in forms of religious practice to which one does not subscribe.

Second, the right not to have certain things done to oneself—not to be killed or imprisoned unjustly, not to be tortured or enslaved, not to be lied to, not to have one's property stolen or one's good name defamed.

Third, the right to have yet other things done for one—a child's right to be nurtured by his or her parents, for example, an aged parent's right to be cared for by children, a worker's right to be paid a fair wage and provided with decent working conditions by his or her employer.[3]

Clearly, though, rights of the second and third kinds make no sense in isolation—apart, that is, from somebody else's obligation. To each and every right like these (to have things done for one, not to have other things done to one) there must be a corresponding duty. Finnis points to the case of Robinson Crusoe to illustrate the point:

> The man shipwrecked and alone on his island and unknown by the rest of the world certainly wants and needs food, shelter, clothing; but it would be empty to express those needs as rights, for we can point to no one who has any duty to provide them for him. He has an abstract right to be rescued, but if there is no one who both knows of his plight and has the means to rescue him, Robinson Crusoe has no actual right worth thinking of, since no person actually has the duty to rescue him.
>
> The concrete content of my right to be provided for exactly corresponds to the concrete content of some identifiable person's duty to make that provision for me. The extent of my right is determined by the extent of the other's duty.[4]

Similarly with the second kind of right, my right not to have certain things done to me corresponds to the obligation that others have not to *do* them. And even with the first, my right to do some things corresponds to the duty of others to allow me to do them, as my right not to do things corresponds to a duty of other people not to make me do them.

All of which points to a basic, essential fact about "rights talk" generally: rights are real if—but *only* if—there are duties that correspond to them. Claiming "rights" that no one else has an obligation to acknowledge and respect makes no sense. (It can be and often is done, of course. No doubt that is why so many claims of "rights" resemble power-grabs more than they do appeals to moral principle.)

Another fundamental distinction regarding rights is that between natural rights and "positive" rights; it is, Germain Grisez says, "of great importance." Natural rights are those arising from human nature—from the fundamental requirements for our fulfillment as human persons. It is never allowable to violate them (though in some cases they admit of exceptions, which are not, strictly speaking, violations). Positive rights, by contrast, are those bestowed by a lawgiver or external authority competent to identify and assign rights in a particular community or social group. They may be set aside (though not casually or unfairly) when the needs of the community itself require doing so.

Take a simple example. Everyone has a natural right to form and express his or her conscientious judgment on public issues. But ordinarily, without a police parade permit, people do not have a right to tie up traffic by marching down the middle of a busy city street at rush hour waving banners and shouting slogans on behalf of their views. To hold and express responsible opinions is a natural right; to parade on the public streets in most cases is a right only for those who have sought and received permission from the appropriate authorities.

A third distinction, closely akin to the second, concerns absolute rights (and duties) on the one hand and those that are real but not absolute on the other.

To be sure, an "absolute" right is one which it is never morally allowable to violate (and to which, of course, an absolute duty—*not* to violate it—corresponds). But what are these rights (and duties), and what makes them absolute—that is, never to be violated? The answer supplied by natural-law thinkers like Grisez and Finnis is that these entities are expressions, in moral terms, of fundamental elements of our personhood that, taken together, sum up our capacity for fulfillment as the kind of beings we are. Call them basic human goods: fundamental purposes of human action such as life, truth, friendship, play, and religion (for example, a harmonious relationship with God). Grisez says these are "aspects of persons, not realities apart from persons"; they are not "mere outcomes one wants and seeks" but "aspects of... human 'full-being.'"[5]

Considered in the moral terms of right and duty, Finnis says the principle that basic aspects of human well-being are never to be directly suppressed is "the principle of the natural law which gives substance to talk about human dignity, and which provides the rational basis for, or explanation of, the *absolute* moral norms and the *absolute* human rights."[6]

It follows, then, that "non-absolute" rights and duties are those that can be overridden or set aside when circumstances warrant. But that does not mean they are trivial or can casually be ignored.

For example, my boss has a real right to expect me to get to work on time; I have a real duty to do so. Still, my employer's non-absolute right and my non-absolute duty must give way in the face of more pressing rights and duties, either those of an absolute kind (I'm very late one day because the police, responding to a bad accident, had closed the highway out where I live to all but emergency traffic, and I would have had to lie to pass off my drive to work as an emergency) or those that are non-absolute (I'm a little late this morning because I helped a neighbor jump-start his car). Again, I have a genuine right to free speech. But that right, as has been pointed out time and again, does not extend to shouting "Fire!" as a practical joke in a crowded theater.

As Finnis remarks, absolute rights are "unqualified, fully specified," but non-absolute rights "need to be fully specified and qualified so as to take into account the circumstances." That means we need to know more about the circumstances before we can say that in *this* particular case a non-absolute right does (or doesn't) apply. But that points to an obvious question: How is this "specifying" to be done? How are various claims of right to be sorted out and evaluated? The answer: "In the final analysis it is done by holding in one's mind's eye some vision of good life in community."[7]

In other words: the common good.

INDIVIDUAL RIGHTS AND THE COMMON GOOD

We have encountered the common good several times before in this book. Now we need to examine the notion more closely. Only by understanding what it means can we understand rights and responsibilities in any community, including the community called the Catholic Church.

What, in general, is the common good? The Second Vatican Council, mirroring the tradition of Catholic social doctrine, uses the expression many times. As we have seen, its definition, provided in the *Constitution on the Church in the Modern World*, is this: "The common good embraces the sum of those conditions of social life by which individuals, families, and groups can achieve their own fulfillment in a relatively thorough and ready way."

Germain Grisez, using more technical language, says: "The common good of a particular society is the set of basic human goods insofar as members of that society are commonly committed to them and pursue them by cooperative action."[8] The common good, we might say, is composed of the elements of authentic human fulfillment that a community's members resolve to seek together.

According to some accounts of the common good, the good of persons is subordinate to the good of societies; people can be sacrificed when the community's needs and interests require it. That, for instance, was Aristotle's idea of the relationship of individuals to political society. It is unacceptable from the Christian perspective, ruled out by the God-given dignity of human persons that is a central part of the Christian tradition itself.

Thus St. Thomas Aquinas, indebted to Aristotle in so many ways, rejected Aristotle's opinion on this matter. "For Thomas," Grisez points out, "human persons are not ordered to political society according to all they have and are, but rather to God.... [And] faith teaches that subordination to divine goodness requires not the destruction of persons but their fulfillment. Hence, in Catholic social teaching, passages abound in which the primacy of persons is declared."[9] Any attempt to understand the implications of rights and responsibilities must start and end with that fact, so central to the notion of the common good itself.

What is the correct relationship between the individual and the community? When society's interests clash with personal interests, which take precedence? What happens when the rights of individuals come into conflict with the common good?

The Church's social doctrine has wrestled with such questions for a long time. Its fundamental answer, as we have just seen, is that the individual person comes first. But this priority may not be understood in individualistic, much less selfish, terms.

Catholic social teaching expresses a profound abhorrence of totalitarianism, the "anthill society," and whatever subjugates the individual person to the interests of some larger collectivity. In part, this reflects the Church's long struggle throughout much of the twentieth century against fascism and communism. But social doctrine also embodies no less sharp a rejection of individualism, selfishness, and all forms of laissez-faire exploitation of the weak by the strong.

Abstract principles like these do not settle hard cases of conflict between the individual and the community, but they do indicate the parameters within which morally correct solutions must be sought. The ideal relationship is indicated in, for example, Vatican II's *Constitution on the Church in the Modern World:* "The beginning, the subject and the goal of all social institutions is and must be the human person," it declares. But then, a little later on: "Profound and rapid changes make it particularly urgent that no one, ignoring the trend of events or drugged by laziness, content himself with a merely individualistic morality" (*Gandium et Spes,* 30).

This line of thought resolves the tension between the individual person and the social group in a relatively simple manner. The community exists for the person, but the person must spend himself or herself in serving others and promoting the common good of all. Thus from time immemorial soldiers who risk their lives in defense of the homeland, as well as doctors, nurses, and relief workers who put themselves at risk at the scene of a disaster have been praised and honored for their service to the common good.

Several basic convictions underlie this approach: For example, the conviction that the human person is social by nature; people must live together and interact, not just to survive but to fulfill their human potential in all ways. Another conviction is expressed in the principle of subsidiarity: That which can be done successfully on a lower level of social organization should not be done at a higher level; but the higher level *is* responsible for what needs doing but cannot be done on the lower level. (This way of proceeding encourages and supports a network of free, interacting social agents and institutions, extending from the individual person through family, church, and neighborhood, all the way to the level of relationships among nations. In the American context, the traditional strong emphasis on local control of schools is a typical expression of subsidiarity at work.) Catholic social doctrine also recognizes such complementary principles as "socialization" and "interdependence," concepts that take into account the complexity of modern social and economic life and assign important roles to social structures, including government. Thus, to a great extent, the contemporary emphasis on the duties of rich nations to poor ones arises from a heightened appreciation of interdependence.

Pope John Paul II expresses a strong personalist emphasis throughout his writings on social themes. His very first encyclical, *The Redeemer of Man* (*Redemptor Hominis*, published in 1980), stresses the "unique unrepeatable human reality" of the individual. In this view, social policy and the actions of communities always must be evaluated by their impact on individuals and not just by how well they serve the interests of some group (even if that "group" happens to be in the majority).

By no means, however, does this individual emphasis exclude social concern and sensitivity to the common good of all. That is clear, for example, in the pope's analysis of human freedom, where he rejects a view of individual liberty that amounts to do-as-you-please: "Nowadays it is sometimes held, though wrongly, that freedom is an end in itself, that each human being is free when he makes use of freedom as he wishes, and that this must be our aim in the lives of individuals and societies. In reality, freedom is a great gift only when we know how to use it consciously for everything that is our true good. Christ teaches us that the best use of freedom is charity, which takes concrete form in self-giving and in service" (*Redemptor Hominis,* 21).

For Pope John Paul "solidarity" is a key to social morality. He explains it as a virtue that gives rise to ethically correct responses to the fact of social and economic interdependence. It is an obvious fact of life today that individuals and even whole societies are linked in a multitude of ways; and this fact is not just a piece of sociological (or economic or political) data but a reality with profound moral consequences. As such, it should guide relationships among individuals, groups and even nations. "Solidarity helps us to see the 'other'—whether a person, people or nation—not just as some kind of instrument, with a work capacity and physical strength to be exploited at low cost and then discarded when no longer useful, but as our 'neighbor,' a 'helper'... to be made a sharer, on a par with ourselves, in the banquet of life to which all are equally invited by God."

To repeat, such principles have a bearing on the exercise of rights and the fulfillment of responsibilities in any society. Specifically, they are relevant to rights and responsibilities in the Church. Even in our familiar Holy Family Parish there is a dense network of human relationships, a set of shared values and commitments, an authentic "common good." This is not the pastor's fiefdom, nor is it a setting for intra-parish competition among various interest groups (the "school people" versus the "CCD people," say, or the retirees versus the young singles). It is a community of *Christifidelis*—Christ's faithful people—all of whom are called by their very identity as such to work harmoniously to realize the purposes binding them together as part of the body of Christ.

THE COMMON GOOD OF THE CHURCH

The Church is profoundly different from any other society. She is a unique community in which the first and most important dimension of "communion" is humankind's covenantal communion in and through Jesus Christ with God. Because the Church is unique, it is a mistake to suppose simplistically that everything in social doctrine applies directly and unequivocally to her.

Yet the Church also is (though not exclusively) a real human society, a "people," in which there are real human relationships involving duties and rights. That explains the need for canon law itself. The members of the Church fulfilled in heaven will have no differences of opinion or conflicting interests; but the *Christifideles* pursuing their pilgrim way as the Church on this earth often do not see eye to eye. Thus they need many of the same checks and balances and norms governing life in common that any human society needs in order to avoid or resolve conflicts and function reasonably well.

As Pope John Paul points out in the apostolic constitution introducing the revised Code: "Since the Church is organized as a social and visible structure, it must also have norms: in order that its hierarchical and organic structure be visible; in order that the exercise of the functions divinely entrusted to it, especially that of sacred power and of the administration of the sacraments, may be adequately organized; in order that the mutual relations of the faithful may be regulated according to justice based upon charity, with the rights of individuals guaranteed and well-defined; in order, finally, that common initiatives undertaken to live a Christian life ever more perfectly may be sustained, strengthened, and fostered by canonical norms."

Lest there be any doubt about the matter, Canon 223 makes it clear that there is such a thing as a "common good of the Church." Individuals and groups of the faithful are instructed to take this common good into account in exercising their rights. Further, the Church's pastoral leaders are said to have the authority to regulate the exercise of rights by her members "in the interest of the common good." Evidently, the Church's common good is the norm or standard for claiming rights and assigning duties.

"Very well," someone might say, "then what is this 'common good of the Church' by which rights and responsibilities are measured? What aspects or elements of human fulfillment do the members of this unique community called 'Church' commit themselves to pursue and realize together?"

The obvious answer is, of course: quite a few. After all, the "common good" of any community is not just one good but many. It is a range of basic human goods or purposes, for the sake of whose realization in its members the community exists. That also is true of the Church.

Thus a broad spectrum of human goods belong to, or at least touch upon, the Church's common good. Many are identified as rights and responsibilities in the Code of Canon Law. They include, for example, free speech and public opinion (Canon 212), association (Canon 215), education in the faith and the pursuit of religious truth (Canon 217), good name and privacy (Canon 220), legal self-defense and due process (Canon 221), the nurture of children (Canon 226). The list could be extended, but the point is clear: Many human goods pertain in some way to the common good of the Church.

Typically, however, a particular community is especially dedicated to the realization in its members of a limited number of human goods or, perhaps, one special good. That helps give the community its distinctiveness, its particular character. For instance, "friendship" in the case of a social club; a good we might call "sport" in the case of a high school basketball team;

"truth" in the case of an academic community. That some social clubs, school teams, and universities neglect or even violate purposes like these for the sake of limited goals like self-gratification or fame or power merely underlines the unpleasant fact that communities, like the individuals who compose them, can and sometimes do jump the track. They abandon commitment to the human goods they are intended to serve.

All this applies to the Church. This unique community of faith exists above all for the realization in her members of a particular human good. Its name is (to use Grisez's terminology) religion.

Often, when people speak of "religion," they mean "organized religion"—in other words, the network of institutions, structures, and systems within various denominations and church groups. Others mean by religion a subjective and more or less incommunicable personal experience of some kind. These are limited yet legitimate uses of the term. But they aren't what is meant by religion here.

In this context, "religion" refers to a relationship—the relationship of human beings with God (or with whomever or whatever fills the place of God in the worldview of a particular individual or group: the Transcendent Other, the Spirit of the Universe, or possibly even the Dialectic of History). Human persons and human cultures in every time and place have cultivated, and continue to cultivate, a harmonious relationship with whatever occupies this place in their scheme of things.

The basic human good of religion, Germain Grisez says, is that harmonious relationship with God that perfects human persons as persons.[10] For Catholics and other religious believers in the Judeo-Christian tradition, there is no question about whom this relationship concerns: the God of Abraham and Isaac, the God of the Old and New Covenants, the God whom Jesus Christ addresses, and tells us to address, as Father. The meaning of covenant itself—and therefore the meaning of Jesus' covenant-forming life and death—is found in harmonious human relations, a relationship of love, with this God. That is the human good of religion, which the Church especially exists to foster and sustain in her members. Jesus speaks of it as "the kingdom," which he announced and told us to "seek first."

Not, however, merely individualistically—"me and God," as it were. In fact, this good called religion cannot be fully realized by human beings in isolation from one another. A harmonious relationship with God is inseparable from harmonious relationships with other human persons. It is bound up with life within the community of the Church. When, as sometimes happens at Holy Family (and in many other parishes, if the truth be told), the sign of peace during the Eucharistic celebration is only a superficial gesture on the part of people who in reality are indifferent—and in some cases even hostile—to one another, the authenticity of their worship is itself open to question.

St. Paul tells the Christians of Corinth: "Let no one seek his own good, but the good of his neighbor" (1 Cor 10:24). This seeking the good of one's neighbor is not just a matter of "being nice," nor is it even simply a matter of humanitarian concern for the well-being of others (as desirable and important as that practical concern is). Rather, in the communion of the Church, seeking the neighbor's good is inextricably bound up with the relationship with God.

Many passages in the New Testament underline that fact. As the First Epistle of John puts it: "If any one has the world's goods and sees his brother in need, yet closes his heart against him, how does God's love abide in him?… If any one says, 'I love God,' and hates his brother, he is a liar" (1 Jn 3:17, 4:20). And, of course, this practical concern for the well-being of others also, and especially, is directed to their spiritual welfare. St. Paul makes this dramatically clear: "I try to please all men in everything I do, not seeking my own advantage, but that of many, that they may be saved. Be imitators of me, as I am of Christ" (1 Cor 10:33-11:1).

Even though commitment to the basic human good called religion gives the community of faith its distinctive character, it does not follow that, within the Church, other human goods may be sacrificed to this one.

In any social context, the essence of fanaticism consists in supposing that one basic human good takes such precedence over others that the others can be violated for its sake. In the religious context, fanaticism is rooted in this view of the good of religion: hence the long, sorry history of religious persecution inflicted on one group by another, of repeated violations of human rights and decency in the name of "religion"—of holy wars, martyrdoms, and outrages of all kinds. This history continues up to the present day—in the Protestant-Catholic conflict in Northern Ireland, in parts of Africa and the Arab world where militant Islam strives to stamp out Christianity, and in other places as well.

Over the centuries such behavior on the part of religious people has had the effect of discrediting religion itself in the eyes of many. Tracing the rise of contemporary atheism in part to the misdeeds of religious believers, the Second Vatican Council remarked: "To the extent that they neglect their own training in the faith, or teach erroneous doctrine, or are deficient in their religious, moral, or social life, they must be said to conceal rather than reveal the authentic face of God and religion" (*Gaudium et Spes,* 19). Religious fanaticism—violating human goods in the name of the good of religion—is such an act of concealment.

In fairness, though, we shouldn't think that religious fanaticism is the only kind. Fanaticism is possible in the pursuit of any human good—health (think of diet freaks and exercise nuts), knowledge (consider scholars who sacrifice family life, friendship, recreation, and just about everything else to their single-minded pursuit of esoteric knowledge), or whatever it may be. A journalist who worked for many years at a major American daily newspaper once told me of a staff meeting at which a senior editor informed the assembled journalists that they did well not to affiliate with a church or synagogue, lest they suffer divided loyalties—a clear case of fanaticism in the cause of the news business.

Fanaticism also can pervert relationships *within* the Church. In the Church, too, the notion that some rights (or the rights of some) can be violated or suppressed in the name of a "higher good" must be excluded. Such an attitude can be a real temptation, especially for people in positions of religious authority. It helps account for a long train of private tragedies and public scandals, from sidetracked careers and lives ruined (at least by human standards) to grave abuses in the use of contributed funds and property and repeated failures to practice accountability. Even Holy Family's Monsignor Hellman, a decent man at heart, has been known to fire a church custodian with a family upon finding someone else who'd work cheaper. "Can't waste the parish's money," he would explain, certain he was doing the right thing.

The enumeration of rights and responsibilities in the Code of Canon Law excludes such abuses. The Code leaves no doubt as to the essential mission of the Church. Canon 747 expresses it this way: "The Church, to whom Christ the Lord entrusted the deposit of faith so that, assisted by the Holy Spirit, it might reverently safeguard revealed truth, more closely examine it and faithfully proclaim and expound it, has the innate duty and right to preach the gospel to all nations...."

But in order for this mission to be carried out, the rights of the Church's members must be respected and they must fulfill their duties in their diverse, specific ways. As "sharers in Christ's priestly, prophetic and royal office in their own manner," Canon 204 declares, the Christian faithful are "called to exercise the mission which God has entrusted to the Church to fulfill in the world, in accord with the condition proper to each one." The Church's mission is accomplished through the exercise of their rights and the fulfillment of their duties by her members.

Especially the accomplishment of the Church's mission requires living witness in the relationships among her members to such virtues and values as friendship, justice, and charity. The Church, Vatican II teaches, was established by Christ as a community in which "everyone, as members one of the other, would render mutual service according to the different gifts bestowed upon each"; the Church is the community in which "we serve each other unto salvation." Rights and duties in the Church should only be understood and exercised in this light.

FOREGOING RIGHTS

Justice is fundamental to Christian life, but charity is more fundamental still. "All things considered," Germain Grisez remarks, "Catholic moral theology and social teaching should be cautious in using the language of rights. In reading the New Testament, one finds a great deal about the responsibilities of Christians, very little about rights."[11] That points to another special feature of the rights of Christians: namely, that Christians very often are called to forego—voluntarily to give up—their claims to rights. Charity, not justice, is at the center of Christian life.

Justice is a virtue of great importance in social relationships of all kinds. In particular, to the extent that justice signifies a responsibility that I have to other people—*my* obligation to give *others* their due—it is a grave duty to be just. But justice also can be understood from the point of view of self-interest and personal right—*my* claim upon others to give me my due. It is then that, very often, Christians should look to a higher virtue, charity, and give up their claim to rights.

In his 1980 encyclical on the mercy of God (*Dives in Misericordia*), Pope John Paul gives a striking analysis of the respective roles of justice and charity for Christians, simply in ordinary life. In a section called "Is Justice Enough?" he makes it clear that the Church shares the desire of people today for "a life which is just in every respect." But, he goes on to say, very often programs and projects committed in their inception to the pursuit of justice come in the course of time to "suffer from distortions." He explains:

> Although they continue to appeal to the idea of justice, nevertheless experience shows that other negative forces have gained the upper hand over justice, such as spite, hatred, and even cruelty.... It is obvious, in fact, that in the name of an alleged justice (for example, historical justice or class justice) the neighbor is sometimes destroyed, killed, deprived of liberty, or stripped of fundamental human rights. The experience of the past and of our own time demonstrates that justice alone is not enough, that it can even lead to the negation and destruction of itself, if that deeper power, which is love, is not allowed to shape human life in its various dimensions. Dives in Misericordia, 12

All this is true, as the Pope points out, as a matter of painful, practical experience in ordinary life. But for Christians the challenge to put love before justice arises from a deeper source and is a more compelling duty. As is always the case in Christian life, the model is supplied by Christ himself. The letter to the Philippians spells it out:

> Do nothing from selfishness or conceit, but in humility count others better than yourselves. Let each of you look not only to his own interests, but also to the interests of others. Have this mind among yourselves, which was in Christ Jesus, who, though he was in the form of God, did not count equality with God a thing to be grasped, but emptied himself, taking the form of a servant, being born in the likeness of men. And being found in human form he humbled himself and became obedient unto death, even death on a cross. Philippians 2:3-8

Some people will object to the point I am making. "You can't be serious. What you are describing isn't just impractical—it's immoral. People who forego their rights aren't merely denying themselves what they're entitled to. Very often, such misguided generosity can harm other people to whom they have serious obligations.

"When they're laying off workers in a factory, should a husband and father with seniority *not* claim his right to keep his job, out of consideration for somebody who's been there a shorter time? That might be very noble of him, but it would be grossly unfair to his wife and children.

"Or, if a peaceful country is attacked without warning by an aggressive one, should its ruler decline to fight back, on the grounds that he is foregoing the right of self-defense? If so, the ruler would be betraying his people's trust. He should be removed from office, not praised.

"The same thing holds true in the Church. For instance, a bishop has a right to be chief teacher of the faith in his diocese. If somebody challenges his authority by teaching heresy as Christian truth, the bishop should exercise his authority. If he fails to do that, he is failing to do what a bishop should."

These objections, and others like them, make an important point. People who forego rights aren't always doing the right thing. In the examples cited, those tempted to surrender their rights would fail in their duty to others by doing so—to his family in the case of the overly obliging factory worker, to the citizens of his country in the case of the negligent ruler, to the people of his diocese in the case of the permissive bishop.

Evidently, Christians need a further principle for deciding when it is morally correct to forego their rights and when it is not. That principle, says Grisez, is personal vocation: "Christians... must seek and accept everything as a gift from God. In imitation of Jesus, who did not cling to his right to divine honor, they ought to prefer others' interests in preference to their own.... Christians therefore ought not to be concerned about their rights but about the responsibilities entailed by their personal vocations.... Christians should seek to vindicate their rights when this is required to fulfill their responsibilities, but not otherwise."[12]

SOURCES OF RIGHTS AND RESPONSIBILITIES IN THE CHURCH

Some responsibilities and rights, as we have seen, come from human nature. Some come from law, contract, social custom, and other similar external sources. Where do the responsibilities and rights of Christians come from? The answer is: From all of these sources and also from several others— namely, the sacraments, the hierarchical structure of the Church, and personal vocation.

Pope John Paul makes the sacramental source of rights and responsibilities very clear: "The participation of the lay faithful in the threefold mission of Christ as Priest, Prophet and King"—and therefore the duties and rights that accompany such participation—"finds its source in the anointing of Baptism, its further development in Confirmation and its realization and dynamic sustenance in the Holy Eucharist" (*Christifideles Laici*, 14). To this list, we can also add the "state in life" sacraments, Matrimony and Holy Orders, which carry with them very specific duties and rights—many of them spelled out in the Code of Canon Law—that are associated with those "states."

Similarly, the Pope is clear about the hierarchical structure of the Church, with its diverse, complementary offices, roles and functions, as a source of duties and rights. Underlining the "organic" character of ecclesial communion ("analogous to that of a living and functioning body"), he writes: "In fact, at one and the same time it is characterized by a diversity and complementarity of vocations and states in life, of ministries, of charisms and responsibilities. Because of this diversity and complementarity every member of the lay faithful is seen in relation to the whole body and offers a totally unique contribution on behalf of the whole body" (*Christifideles Laici*, 20).

A totally unique contribution.... This is the contribution which each member of the Church is called to make by reason of his or her personal vocation. In practical terms, it takes the form of fulfilling responsibilities and exercising rights, including (but not limited to) those specified in canon law. The idea of personal vocation goes back very far in Christian thinking, but only recently has it been developed in depth. We must reflect upon it deeply in order to have a clear understanding of Christian duties and rights.

For reasons having mainly to do with history, however, that is not such an easy thing to do. Say "vocation" to many Catholics and they think of a calling to the priesthood or religious life. "This parish hasn't produced a vocation in years," Monsignor Hellman sometimes privately complains—meaning that no one has entered the seminary or convent. Father Ross for his part gamely plugs away with Holy Family's young people, trying to fill this "vocations" gap. The priesthood and religious life obviously are vocations of great dignity and importance. But in recent years the Church's understanding of vocation has expanded dramatically to take in more. The message, repeated by Pope John Paul and others, is that *every* Christian, whether priest, religious, or lay person, has a personal vocation uniquely his or her own.

Not only that—Pope John Paul teaches that "personal vocation and mission" are central components of every Catholic's duty to participate in the Church's work according to his or her circumstances. If enough people come to understand, accept and act upon this way of thinking about vocation, it will renew their lives and revolutionize the Church as well as wider society.

PERSONAL VOCATION

I was a long time catching on to that. For years I missed the point that my marriage, my children, my writing, my friends, and multiple associations were elements of my vocation. If I had a "vocation" at all, I more or less supposed, it concerned only what was properly and specifically "religious" in my life. That pretty much limited my vocation to the small amount of time I spent in church. Only gradually and late, through reading and conversation with wise advisers as well as prayer, did I come to realize that my entire life was—or at least was meant to be—a unique share in God's redemptive plan for the world: *my* personal vocation.

The idea of personal vocation is both modern and also very old. It is implicit in the Pauline image of the Church as body of Christ, a unique communion in which each individual member has an unrepeatable role to play for the welfare of all: "For as in one body we have many members, and all the members do not have the same function, so we, though many, are one body in Christ, and individually members one of another. Having gifts that differ according to the grace given to us, let us use them" (Rom 12:4-6).

The same idea appears in many places in the tradition of the Church and especially in the teaching of Vatican II. But it is Pope John Paul in particular who has developed the theological basis for the concept of personal vocation. "From eternity God has thought of us and has loved us as unique individuals," he says. "Every one of us he called by name" (*Christifideles Laici*, 58).

The fact that all members of the Church—laypeople as much as religious and priests—have personal vocations does not cancel out other ways of thinking about vocation. Instead, it deepens and enriches them. In fact, it now appears that the term "vocation" refers to at least three distinct but related realities present in the life of each Christian.

One of these is the common Christian vocation that comes from baptism. Far from being merely a social convention with some religious trappings, baptism is a stupendous event in the life of the one who is "christened," whether he or she be an infant or a mature adult. This is the start of a "new life" in Christ—the life of faith. With this new life comes, inevitably, a divine calling to love and serve God and neighbor and cooperate with Jesus in continuing his work of redemption.

Another meaning of "vocation" is a calling to a particular state in life or a recognized Christian lifestyle. The priesthood and religious life are such "states" and so, by most accounts, is the state of the laity. Especially since Vatican II, the way of life of those living in and living out the sacrament of matrimony also is understood to be a distinct vocation in this particular sense.

The third meaning is unique personal vocation. It includes the first two—common Christian vocation and state in life—and fleshes them out in relation to the special circumstances of the individual Christian's life. It is, as it were, everything that goes into an individual's response to the unique graces God offers him or her, based on the baptismal vocation common to all. I still remember the reaction of a lay woman when I made this point in a talk to a parish group several years ago. "Imagine that—I have a vocation!" she exclaimed, genuinely excited. And with good reason: It is a genuinely exciting idea.

In fact, unique personal vocation is a comprehensive reality inasmuch as it takes in the whole of a person's life. People who see that they have their own unique roles in the divine plan—that God is calling them to do something he has never asked (and never will ask) anyone else to do—naturally are moved to organize their whole lives according to what they discern as God's will for them. That extends from the most important decisions like career and marriage (state in life, that is, now understood as an aspect of one's personal vocation), to the apparently—though often not really—unimportant choices like hobbies and vacations.

But why, someone might ask, aren't little things like hobbies and vacations "unimportant," at least relatively speaking? There are two reasons.

First, because a personal vocation really does take in the whole of life—God's will for each one of us extends to our leisure time and recreation just as much as it does to anything else. Second, because to a greater extent than often is recognized—or at least admitted—people really do shape themselves and their relationships by the choices they make concerning things like vacations and hobbies. So, for instance, a married man's decision about whether to spend a weekend hunting with the guys or camping with the wife and kids may be no small matter—especially if his job has kept him from spending much time with the family lately. This may be a decision by which he either responds to his personal vocation precisely insofar as it *includes* marriage and family life or else walks away from it.

Unique personal vocation also is a potential source of enormous new energy for the Church. In this perspective, the danger that discussions of rights and responsibilities will degenerate into petty power struggles and squabbling over perks and privileges falls away, replaced by fresh, urgent motivation for finding how best one can serve the others in one's life. Pope John Paul lays it on the line: "Each member of the lay faithful should always be fully aware of being a member of the Church yet entrusted with a unique task which cannot be done by another and which is to be fulfilled for the good of all" (*Christifideles Laici*, 28).

But isn't there a danger that stressing unique personal vocation—including the vocation of each lay Catholic—will lead people away from the priesthood and religious life, and so make the "vocations shortage" even worse than it now is?

Start with the fact that the "vocations shortage" is a myth. *There is no shortage of vocations. What is in short supply among*

Catholics is the awareness that everybody has a vocation. If more people took to heart the idea that they need to give serious attention to finding out ("discernment," it is called) what their personal vocations are, there is little doubt that more would discover that their personal vocations include a calling to the priesthood or religious life, while the rest would have a powerful incentive for living as fully committed Christian laypeople.

Germain Grisez has given careful attention to the question of personal vocation. The idea is central to some of his most serious writing on the moral principles that shape Christian life. He rejects the notion that more emphasis on personal vocation will drain off potential candidates for the priesthood and religious life.

"The diverse roles of service to which Christians are called are not like various employers competing for a small group of competent people," he writes. "Rather, each Christian's vocation is a given—an objective state of affairs—to be discerned. If more… were listening for God's call, more would hear it."[13]

Correctly understood, personal vocation offers no encouragement to individualism. It is not an invitation to follow one's subjective whim or inclination, but a call to learn and to do God's will. That is something which we may not find particularly attractive at first, since there's a good chance it will conflict with our own assumptions and prejudices. We almost certainly will find it to be full of surprises as it gradually unfolds.

The key here is discernment—the ongoing process by which a person comes to "see" what God wants of him or her. Pope John Paul says it involves "receptive listening to the Word of God and the Church," sincere and constant prayer, the advice of a wise spiritual director, and a realistic appraisal of one's individual talents and capacities in relation to the needs and opportunities present in the world around one. (See *Christifideles Laici,* 58).

No mere subjective individualism here. Discernment is a process of reality-testing in which Scripture and the teaching and discipline of the Church play key roles, along with personal factors like taste and temperament.

A while back, in connection with a question-and-answer column I write for a Catholic newspaper, I received a moving letter from a man who felt that he might have a calling to the religious life. Unfortunately, he also suffered from a serious, chronic neurological condition. So up to that time he hadn't found a religious congregation willing to accept him as a candidate. He had two questions. Could I suggest a religious community where he might fit in? And, considering his problem, was it possible that he didn't really have a religious vocation at all?

On the first question, I'm afraid I did not help him very much. Keep asking around, I advised, and consult with well-informed people professionally involved in "vocations" work. They can give you more solid, factual advice than I can.

As for his second question, all I could do was express admiration. For here was someone who had a clear and realistic understanding of "vocation"—not what he wanted to do, but what God wanted.

No thanks to me, my correspondent had grasped a profound truth. If God really asks something of us as part of our personal vocations, he also will provide a way for us to do it. Where there is no way—where roadblocks in us or in our surroundings are literally insurmountable—that "something" to which we feel attracted, no matter how noble it may be and no matter how generous our motives, is not truly part of our call.

In this whole area, then, feelings are important but not conclusive. "Thy will be done" is the prayer that must begin and end every honest effort to discern a personal vocation. It goes without saying that it also is the prayer that must guide our efforts to discern our rights as members of the Church, and know when to claim and when to forego them. Our rights and duties as Christians are best understood as means, instruments, for living out our vocations. Whether to claim or to forego a particular right, whether to assume and fulfill a duty: these are questions that followers of Christ can only rightly answer in a vocational context. What has God called me to do? What is the best way of doing it? Only when they are rooted in a firm sense of vocation do Christian responsibilities and rights come into focus.

But Catholic laypeople do face obstacles to exercising the rights and fulfilling the duties of their personal vocations, even when these are correctly discerned as well as (and especially) when they are not. One of the most serious obstacles is clericalism. It is that issue to which we now must turn.

SEVEN

The Problem of Clericalism

G INNIE GILMORE, A CATHOLIC ASSEMBLYWOMAN in her fourth term in the state legislature, describes herself as "personally opposed" to abortion but a supporter of the "right to choose." As such, she consistently votes for pro-abortion legislation. Although she's a prominent member of Holy Family Parish, she explains privately: "The Church can't tell me what to do as an elected public official."

Fred Hightower spent three years in the seminary. Now he's happily married, a successful businessman and father of four. He also is well known in Holy Family, where he's a lector at Mass. Nevertheless, thinking about the old days, he sometimes has the nagging feeling that in not becoming a priest he settled for second-best. "I'm just a layman," he remarks apologetically when religious subjects come up.

Monsignor Thomas Hellman, pastor of Holy Family, has no doubt in his mind that in the parish his word is—and ought to be—law. He has never bothered to set up a parish council ("I know what my people are thinking," he tells other pastors with utter conviction). Older parishioners like Fred Hightower generally have no problem with that. But younger Catholics aren't as visible around Holy Family as they used to be.

These are three very different people, but their stories have a common thread. In their various ways, Ms. Gilmore, Fred Hightower, and Monsignor Hellman are all in the grip of clericalism. None has a proper view of the roles of the laity and clergy in today's Church and world.

They're not the only ones. Clericalism is among the biggest obstacles to the laity's exercise of rights and fulfillment of responsibilities. Clericalism is pervasive and deeply rooted. And it is very nearly invisible to many people, simply because clericalist ways of thinking and acting are so widely taken for granted.

It is not only (and today, perhaps, not even mainly) a problem among priests. I've argued elsewhere that today's American Catholic laity may on the whole be more clericalized than their clergy.[1] Many priests, though certainly not all, have successfully internalized the message of the Second Vatican Council regarding laypeople. But, in many cases, the latter have yet to understand what it means to be partners, equal in dignity to the clergy, in carrying on the mission of the Church.

The clericalist view of the laity has serious consequences. Passivity is one—the attitude expressed, for instance, in Fred Hightower's "...just a layman." A false distinction between one's responsibilities of faith and one's secular roles and duties is another—expressed by Ginnie Gilmore's comment, "The Church can't tell me what to do as an elected public official." The notion that priests give the orders and laypeople obey—Monsignor Hellman's view of things—is a third.

Vatican II deplores the "split" between faith and life, calling it one of the most serious problems among Catholics in our times. Parishes and Church-related institutions across the United States are pining for more lay involvement and vitality, but hardly anybody talks about "apostolate" of the laity in and to the world. Pope John Paul warns against clericalizing the laity—and laicizing the clergy—on the basis of just such clericalist thinking as this.

Whatever may have been true in earlier times, when conditions in Church and society were very different, clericalism is something today's Catholics no longer can afford. Make no mistake about it: we all—clergy, religious, and laity—absolutely must put clericalism behind us, if we are to grasp and live out our duties and our rights as members of the Church.

WHAT EXACTLY IS CLERICALISM?

Clericalism can be defined and explained from a number of different points of view, all of them valid. Historically, for example, clericalism seems to have a lot to do with attitudes toward "the world"—the secular order and the life of ordinary laypeople therein—that emerged for reasons both good and bad in the early centuries of Christianity.

Much of this way of thinking is summed up in a Latin phrase, *contemptus mundi*—contempt for the world. It has a good and valid sense in Christian asceticism. But, understood from a clericalist perspective, *contemptus mundi* very often has signified literal "contempt" for the world, along with a corresponding devaluation of the way of life of those who live and work there—laypeople. Historically, too, clericalist attitudes often have been carried into the political forum, so that in former ages popes and bishops claimed ultimate authority over princes, emperors, and kings, not only in spiritual matters but also in temporal ones. To be sure, the princes, emperors, and kings at the same time were claiming and exercising authority in religious matters. That certainly didn't help. The result, naturally, was centuries of church-state conflict that helped bring about the extreme anticlericalism that marred so much of European history in the eighteenth, nineteenth, and even twentieth centuries.

Leaving all that aside, however, I prefer to focus here on clericalism's relationship to a certain way of thinking about vocation. It comes down to this: the priestly vocation and the clerical lifestyle set the standard for all other vocations and lifestyles in the Church. To be a cleric was seen as the highest expression—the ideal, the norm—of the Christian way of life. Every other vocation, state in life, and Christian lifestyle was judged and evaluated by how closely it approximated the clerical norm. To put it bluntly, the more you looked and acted like a member of the clergy, the better a Christian you were.

The implications for laypeople of this longstanding distorted view are apparent.

For example, in the Western Church, priests do not marry, whereas most laypeople do. If clericalism is correct, it seems to follow that marriage itself is a kind of obstacle to Christian perfection, a commitment that virtually guarantees second-rate spiritual status. And, indeed, there have been times over the centuries when marriage has been thought of in just those terms—as a way of life for second-class Christians, a compromise solution for persons of limited generosity and zeal, a fallback position for the halfhearted and lukewarm.

Again, consider the place of work in the clericalist scheme of things. Along with the duties of marriage and family life, work occupies most of the time of most adult laypeople. Yet it is only very recently, as these things are measured, that much thought has been given to the role of work in the quest for perfection. Previously, work was for the most part thought of as no more than a distraction (and a source of many temptations and occasions of sin) for those who engaged in it—that is, for the laity.

What about sanctity itself? As clericalism sees it, priests (and religious, to the extent they are thought of as being a kind of clerical auxiliary corps) are meant to be holy. Laypeople are meant to save their souls, but that's about all. There's a two-track view of spirituality discernible here. On the sainthood track are priests and religious. The path of spiritual mediocrity is clogged with lay men and women.

The antidote to all this lies in unique personal vocation. What is the norm—the standard, the ideal—for a Christian? The answer is: God's will for him or her. For some, God's will includes a calling to the priesthood or religious life. God plainly calls others to the lay state and all it entails. The way of Christian perfection lies in fidelity to God's will. And for most Catholics such fidelity marks out an unmistakable path to sanctity in the very midst of the secular world, through the conscientious, loving exercise of rights and responsibilities as workers, spouses, and parents.

A lot has happened in recent decades to change and correct the clericalist way of thinking. Vatican II's teaching on the laity was a historic milestone. Milestones, too, were the Synod of 1987 and Pope John Paul's document, *The Lay Members of Christ's Faithful People*. The 1983 Code of Canon Law is of great importance in this story. For, as we have seen, it expresses in canonical terms a whole new way of seeing the Church and her lay members.

Yet clericalist ways of thinking and acting linger on, although today sometimes in disguise.

Certainly they linger on in the passivity, dependency, and alienation of many Catholic laypeople—not all of them, thank God, but many—in their relationship to the Church and the clerical hierarchy. In their very different ways, people like Ginnie Gilmore, Fred Hightower, and Monsignor Hellman testify to the persistence of this problem.

It is a problem that, in the United States today, takes shape in a variety of contexts, expresses itself in a variety of ways. Here I want to speak of two that seem especially corrosive and debilitating: the lack of influence of Catholics upon the political dimension of secular culture; and the confusion about their identity and role apparently experienced by many priests, along with the implications for lay ministry to which such confusion gives rise.

CATHOLICS AND POLITICS

At the present time, Americans who describe themselves as Catholics number around sixty million. Yet who would seriously suggest that authentically Catholic views are reflected in the law on abortion or on government aid to religiously sponsored schools and their students, in the distribution of wealth within society, in relationships among racial and ethnic groups, in public policy on marriage and family life, and in many other matters, to a degree at all proportionate to the influence one might reasonably expect sixty million Americans—one-fourth of the total—to have?

Politically speaking, conservative writer William F. Buckley contends, American Catholics as a group appear to be "an all but inert body of people." Whatever anyone may think about specific current issues and the best way of handling them, the fact is that the Catholic Church, as an organized community within the larger community, lacks an effective voice on most.

That is not to say American Catholics aren't politically successful and influential. Some enjoy very generous helpings of political power and prestige. Yet in all too many cases, Catholic public figures—people like Ginnie Gilmore in our example—support policies profoundly at odds with the moral doctrine of their religious tradition. That they do so with no apparent sense of contradiction between their faith and their political views does not alter that fact. This is a painful instance of the "split" between faith and life—a split with roots in clericalist ways of thinking about both faith *and* life.

Canon 225.2, as we have seen, declares that each lay person is bound by a "special duty" to imbue temporal affairs with the spirit of the gospel, according to his or her particular circumstances and opportunities. Some do. Others do not. Some, it appears, do not even recognize that they have a duty to try.

It's hardly a new problem. John Henry Newman, in a sermon preached in 1832, spoke critically of Christians who "accustom themselves gratuitously to distinguish between their public and private duties, and to judge of them by separate rules." In many instances, the future cardinal said, such people have given in to the temptation of "trusting the world, because it speaks boldly, and thinking that evil must be acquiesced in, because it exists."[2] A century and a half later in the United States, not a few such persons seek our votes at election time, hand down rulings from the benches of our courts, and direct government programs of all kinds. A lot of them are Catholic laypeople.

The problem, though, is not all on the side of the laity. In this whole crucial area of the Christian mission to the world—call it "culture formation" for want of a better term—clerics have largely shoved the laity out of the picture as the ones who speak and act on behalf of gospel values in regard to secular and political questions.

That happens in at least two ways.

The first way is by drawing public attention to clerical pronouncements on social and political matters and away from the informed judgments of Catholic laypeople speaking out of their religious commitment and professional expertise.

A while back, a national magazine quoted a bishop who defended the hierarchy's often very detailed policy declarations on economic justice this way: "The Church has to insert itself into the national debate or else risk finding itself declared—properly—irrelevant." Nobody doubts the truth of that. But it does not follow that the Church addresses questions of economic justice only when bishops and priests have something to say about them. On the contrary, it is properly the responsibility of well-formed and informed Catholic laypeople, speaking and acting in their secular, professional roles, to apply general principles of Catholic social teaching about economic justice to specific contemporary questions.

That suggests the second side of this particular coin. When clerics take over the right and duty that properly belong to laypeople to apply the gospel message to secular issues, not a few laity evidently conclude that this lets them off the hook—that they have no special duty or right in regard to the Church's mission in the secular order. They conclude that it is clerics, not laypeople, who are the Church. The practice reinforces the traditional attitudes and self-understandings of laypeople in a clericalist system.

In order to correct this state of affairs, it is not necessary—indeed, it is not even desirable—that bishops and priests abandon their societal commitments and interests. But they do need to express them differently, in a way genuinely suited to *their* responsibilities and rights as members of the Church. Where Catholic social doctrine is concerned, these can be summed up in two words: *teaching* and *formation*.

Not so long ago, I was party to a conversation involving several representatives of Catholic organizations with legislative and public policy concerns. There was much moaning and groaning about the fact that not many Catholics seem to pay much attention to what such groups say about issues of the day. After listening for a while, I commented as follows:

"Let me call your attention to a distinction that probably isn't made often enough in discussions of this kind—I mean the distinction between teaching social doctrine and making statements on particular current issues. A lot of individuals and groups make a lot of statements on a lot of different issues on behalf of the official Church. That goes on all the time. But I don't see many serious, continuing efforts to teach social doctrine in a comprehensive manner.

"Now, I submit that that's a mistake. It is a case of putting the cart before the horse. In the absence of meaningful exposure to social doctrine, Catholics don't experience this stream of pronouncements on political and economic matters as instructive and edifying. More likely, they experience it as irritating and alienating.

"Surely, after a hundred years, the Church does have an integrated, rich, complex body of principles and norms pertaining to social and political questions. Why not *teach* them? Everyone would be better off if we did."

According to the division of labor within a genuine lay-clergy partnership, *forming* the laity in Catholic doctrine is properly the task of bishops and priests, while *applying* doctrine to complex issues in the secular world is a duty and right proper to laypeople.

To be sure, responding to their personal vocations, individual laypeople also can take a hand in the work of education and formation; priests and religious for their part sometimes may be called to play roles of direct advocacy in the social and political fields. There's no problem with that since unique personal vocation is the key—the immediate, personal, customized norm—for each member of the Church.

For the most part, though, laity and clergy do have distinct but complementary jobs in relation to politics (broadly conceived). These roles—"formation" in the case of clerics, "action" in the case of laypeople—are indeed *proper* to them. Clericalist thinking produces a kind of mental fog preventing us all—laity and clergy alike—from seeing that fundamental fact as clearly as we should. And it contributes to making American Catholics a body of people who are, as William F. Buckley says, "inert" when it comes to applying Catholic values to political life and the transformation of secular culture in the gospel's light.

THE PROBLEM OF PRIESTLY IDENTITY AND LAY MINISTRY

Clericalism also contributes to the confusion that some priests experience regarding priestly identity. It's a large, complicated issue. Here let me simply separate out a few strands with a special bearing on our theme—the role of the laity. For confusion about the identity of priests almost inevitably leads to and interacts with confusion about the identity of laypeople.

When the United States bishops, at one of their general meetings a few years ago, considered a proposal to let lay persons officiate at funeral services where priests are lacking, this question of priestly identity dominated the debate. Bishop after bishop fretted aloud that approving such a plan would send the "wrong signal" regarding their own view of priests. It would muddy the waters on priestly identity and help make an already existing problem worse. The proposal was defeated.

This debate was just one episode in a long story. During the last several decades the priestly identity problem often has been cited as a factor in defections from the priesthood, as well as in the decline in new priestly vocations in the United States and other Western countries. Pope John Paul made just that point in a talk to a World Synod of Bishops on the priesthood held in 1990, three years after the synod on the laity.

But why, someone might ask, should Catholic priests be any more uncertain about their identity than anybody else? That is a large and complicated question which I can't attempt to answer here. Instead, let's consider just a few aspects of an explanation touching on (among other things) this matter of rights, responsibilities, and the laity.

In a sense, the problem of priestly identity can be traced back to Vatican II. Not that the Council caused it; but while it said much of great importance about the role of laypeople (and also about the role of bishops, for that matter), the Council had comparatively little new to say about priests. Moreover, some people contend, certain things the Council said about the laity may unintentionally have sown seeds of subsequent confusion regarding priests.

Vatican II gave renewed emphasis to the "common" or "baptismal" priesthood of all the faithful. Let it be said at once that this is a fundamental insight into the very heart and essence of Christian life. It illuminates the core meaning of membership in the Church, whether it be as a lay person, religious, or priest. And it is a truth that, be it noted, was largely neglected by Catholics for many centuries, in favor of a more or less exclusive emphasis upon *ordained* priesthood.

Now, at Vatican II, this insight rooted in the New Testament—that all members of the Church participate in some manner in the priesthood of Christ—was dusted off and brought to the fore. The Council incorporated the idea of the priesthood of the faithful into its vision of the Church as a communion, the people of God. A renewed appreciation of this baptismal priesthood in which all share is one of the Council's great gifts to the Church in our times—a gift deserving far more recognition and appreciation than it has received up to now. (The "priesthood of the faithful" is not the subject of many homilies in Holy Family Parish—or most other parishes either. If it were, Fred Hightower and others like him might feel differently about being "only a layperson.")

At the same time, of course, in the *Constitution on the Church*, Vatican II was at pains to underline another basic fact: ordained priesthood and non-ordained priesthood are essentially different from each other—different "in essence and not only in degree." That was crucial. But perhaps it was not enough. In any case, recognition of the priesthood of all the faithful had the unintended effect of somewhat obscuring the specific identity of *ordained* priests.

Further complicating the situation in the years since Vatican II, it seems, has been a new emphasis, associated with the Council, upon "lay ministries." In saying this, I don't wish to be misunderstood. The participation of laypeople in Church ministries of various kinds unquestionably is a good and commendable thing.

As a practical matter, there is a clear need for laypeople to do some of the work ordinarily done by clergy wherever there are not enough priests to go around. (And that, unfortunately, is likely to be the case in more places in this and some other countries in the years just ahead. As this is written, the number of priests in the United States is about fifty thousand, and it is destined to drop further as an inevitable result of the dearth of new priestly vocations in recent years.) Moreover, as we have seen, Canon 230 of the Code of Canon Law specifically affirms the right of qualified lay persons to share in certain ministries and ministerial functions of a liturgical nature. The good will, generosity, and zeal of the many laity who have responded to the Church's invitation to serve in this way need no demonstrating or defending by me.

But there are problems. One problem, noted earlier, is the undesirable and fundamentally clericalist message that an overemphasis (or a false emphasis) on lay ministries implicitly sends. What message? That *this* way of participating in the life and work of the Church is the best and highest way for genuinely committed laypeople.

Perhaps lay ministry really is the best and highest way for those laity whose personal vocations call them to it. But lay ministry is only for some; whereas all laypeople, without exception, are called to take part in the apostolate in and to the secular world—the world of family, workplace, and neighborhood. For the vast majority of laypeople, this apostolate is central to their vocations. Furthermore, it is the role in the mission of the Church that is proper to them as laity, according to Vatican II and the Code of Canon Law (Canon 225).

The rise of lay ministry also interacts with the difficulties concerning identity experienced by some priests. The more laypeople engage in ministry, it seems, the less certain some members of the clergy become about who *they* are and what *their* job is. Of course, that may be because there was a good deal of fuzzy thinking about priestly identity in the first place: at times priesthood may have been linked to functions and roles (for example, the exercise of temporal and even political authority) that, as we now see clearly, were surely *not* of its essence. Indeed, even within the Church, according to the clericalist model, priests were the only autonomously *active* parties, while laypeople were—and were expected to be—*pas-sive*. It is easy to see how lay ministry can be unsettling to persons in whom, consciously or not, this clericalist mentality persists.

Central to the idea of lay ministry is the notion that laypeople, too, can and should be active in religious roles and settings—notably the liturgy—that formerly were reserved to clerics. Indeed, lay ministry has at times seemed to cover so much ground that priests could be pardoned for wondering exactly what was left, besides offering Mass and hearing confessions, that was proper to the ordained priesthood.

I repeat: this is not the place to try to work out all the problems associated with the priestly identity crisis. My point is merely that lay ministries, good as they are, can raise—and have raised—certain difficulties for priests as well as laypeople. For the latter, as Pope John Paul remarks, the great danger comes down to this: "Being so strongly interested in Church services and tasks that [they] fail to become actively engaged in their responsibilities in the professional, social, cultural, and political world" (*Christifideles Laici*, 2).

If, then, "ministry" is not the way for all laypeople—what is? The answer, in very general terms, is simple: apostolate in and to the secular world. That mainly is how the Catholic laity are meant to exercise their rights and fulfill their responsibilities as members of the Church and participate in the Church's mission. It is time now to consider in some detail what that means, with Pope John Paul II as our guide.

EIGHT

Laity in the World

S OME PEOPLE IN HOLY FAMILY PARISH take a sound, non-clericalist view of the laity's role in the Church, including their relationship to the clergy. For instance:

Kathleen O'Brien, a forty-two-year-old wife and mother of five, is thoroughly comfortable with her identity and lifestyle, which she views in vocational terms. Neither feminist nor anti-feminist, she expects to return to her career as a CPA when her children are older, but right now she considers caring for them and managing a household to be very important work indeed—work that God wants her to do. As a Catholic, further-more, she respects her priests but doesn't kowtow to them. "They have their job to do," she says, "and I have mine."

Kathleen's husband, Jim, regards his work as an attorney as much more than just a way of making money, though his prac-tice unquestionably is a thriving one. Over the years he's done a lot of *pro bono* work for the pro-life movement, including defending several abortion clinic protestors. He considers his profession to be a way of putting his most deeply held beliefs and values to work in the service of others. Busy as he is, though, Jim makes it a point to get home on time and help Kathleen with the kids. Husbanding and fathering also are definitely part of God's plan for him as he sees it.

Father Tom Ross, Holy Family's associate pastor, is something of a transitional figure, even though he hardly thinks of himself that way. On the other hand, vestiges of clericalism are apparent in the way he speaks of "vocation" (he means a calling to be a priest or religious only); on the other hand, his determined efforts to provide meaningful *formation* for lay parishioners (Bible study, adult education) suggest a sound appreciation of the difference between his role and theirs. Father Ross likes being a priest, but he also sincerely admires people like the O'Briens for their faith-filled commitment to family life and work. That, he thinks, is very much the role of well-formed Catholic laypeople today, and very much the outcome that priests like himself should be working to bring about.

He is right. Canon 225.2 of the Code of Canon Law says Catholic laypeople have a particular duty to "imbue and perfect the order of temporal affairs with the spirit of the gospel." By performing their secular duties, the laity give a special kind of witness to Jesus Christ—the witness that is properly theirs to give.

There is no one best way of doing this, no single occupation or secular pursuit that is the preferred way for everybody. All professions and occupations, all kinds of activities, all secular settings and environments, need to be imbued and perfected with the spirit of the gospel. All require the presence and the involvement of committed Christians. It is their witness, both individual and collective, that will transform society and restore the world to God in Christ. Participation in this work of transforming and restoring is not something in addition to each layperson's personal vocation but an essential element of it.

Granted that fundamental fact, nevertheless, someone with specifically vocational and professional decisions to make (What shall I major in in college? What profession or kind of work shall I take up?) is entitled—and even obliged—to weigh his or her particular talents and tastes in relation to certain broad areas of special need in the contemporary world.

Pope John Paul II lists eight of these in his document on the laity. In considering them, we must bear in mind that they represent serious challenges to laypeople. Those who accept these challenges can expect rough going somewhere down the line. Many forces in contemporary secular society operate *against* the gospel's view of human life and the right ordering of society itself. Laity who wish to pay heed to what the Holy Father says—as all should—have their work cut out for them. Why not? No one ever said being a Christian was meant to be easy.

What follows is not intended to be a complete treatment of any one of these eight areas. I only wish to offer a few general thoughts, in the hope of encouraging creative thinking on the part of readers. What can each of us *do* in concrete, practical terms? How does my personal vocation direct me? That's something each of us must decide individually. Pope John Paul provides guideposts, not a road map. We need to find the way for ourselves. But we all need to begin by understanding where the challenge lies.

1. PROMOTING THE DIGNITY OF THE PERSON

The Pope calls this the "central and unifying task" that the Church and her lay members are called to perform for the sake of the human family today. Defending the unique dignity and inviolability of the human person is fundamental to protecting human rights of all kinds. Among other things, it's of central importance to resisting and repelling totalitarianism.

Someone might say that this concern is understandable,

even commendable, on the part of a Polish pope with firsthand experience of Nazi and communist oppression, but has little or no relevance here and now in these democratic United States after the fall of communism and the end of the Cold War. That's a comfortable thought, but it's wrong. Human dignity and rights are violated in many ways, even in this liberal democratic society of ours. (We shall be looking at some of these shortly.)

Even so, what are individuals supposed to do? Maybe social reformers and activists laboring on behalf of good causes can make a difference by righting wrongs, correcting abuses, and shaping a better world. But most of us don't fall into those categories. Is this "central and unifying task" that the pope speaks of, therefore, one to which most people have nothing concrete to contribute?

Not really. To be sure, the contributions that most of us can make are less visible than those of the social reformers and activists (who, however, are by no means always on the morally correct side of issues). But that does not make our contributions any less real. In everyday life, it comes down to this: How do I deal with other people? And how do the positions I take and the decisions I make affect them?

Not people in the abstract—not social classes, races, and groups—but the individual human beings with whom, one by one, I come in contact in the course of a day, in what usually are quite routine, undramatic circumstances: the annoying customer who can't make up his mind, the student who forgot her homework (I, her teacher, know she has family trouble at home), the elderly neighbor who stops me on my walk and bends my ear about nothing in particular longer than I care to have it bent.

It's more than just saying, "Have a nice day," although even that trite remark is a place to start and better than nothing. Everyone is aware of the enormous difference between people who deal with other people as persons and those who deal with them as objects, numbers—*things*.

Doctor Blake, a busy internist and a Holy Family parishioner, gives each of her patients her complete attention and manages to seem really interested in each one because she really is. Her fellow-parishioner, Doctor Heath, equally busy, conveys the impression that he's heard it all before and merely wants to get to the next person in his crowded waiting room. Both are talented, hard-working physicians. Which would you rather have as your doctor? And which one is doing more to promote "the dignity of the person"? The questions pretty much answer themselves.

People in some lines of work—sales, for instance—are coached to smile and be agreeable since that increases customer satisfaction. But all of us have many occasions in our daily lives to treat others with genuine respect and charity, sometimes even in circumstances where doing so can rightly be called heroic. A while back, a token seller in the New York subway was written up in the papers for his cheerful way of greeting each purchaser. Isn't it troubling that such an obvious way of saluting the dignity of persons was also deemed unusual enough to merit media attention? Apparently we take for granted the experience of being reduced to "objects" or "numbers" in our everyday encounters with others.

"As an individual," the Pope says, "a person is not a number or simply a link in a chain, nor even less, an impersonal element in some system" (*Christifideles Laici,* 37). Each of us has opportunities many times a day to give concrete testimony to our belief—or our disbelief—in that.

2. RESPECTING THE INVIOLABLE RIGHT TO LIFE

The right to life, Pope John Paul points out, is the "most basic and fundamental" human right—indeed, it is "the condition" for enjoying all other rights of a human person. It has been grossly violated in many places throughout much of the twentieth century—think of Hitler's Holocaust, Stalin's geno-cidal social policies and prison camps, and the Khmer Rouge "killing fields" in Cambodia. It is also grossly violated in the United States and many other countries today.

Abortion is the most visible instance. Before the campaign for legalized abortion got underway in earnest in the early 1960s, it was universally acknowledged that the unborn being in the womb is a unique human individual in the process of growth and development (a process, incidentally, continuing long after birth as well as before). Only after abortion became the litmus test in a frenzied ideological campaign conducted under the banner of "choice" was this elementary, biologically verified fact systematically ignored, denied, and swept under the rug. Yet denying the right to life of the unborn does not eliminate that right. It merely applies rhetorical salve to the consciences of those who wish to violate it.

Predictably, of course, abortion is no longer the only area in which the right to life is threatened and attacked today. The lives of the elderly, the terminally ill, and those deemed to have a diminished "quality" of life because of mental or physical handicap are threatened by euthanasia and the drive for its legalization under various names such as "assisted suicide." Life is a continuum. Approve its violation at one point, and its violation elsewhere, in another context, becomes that much easier. Pope John Paul and others speak of an encroaching "culture of death." Its signs are visible all around us.

Here, too, the question is: What can individuals do? In fact, quite a lot. The pro-life movement is a multifaceted effort embracing activities of many kinds. Some people have the knowledge and expertise for effective efforts in the arena of law and public policy. Others can participate in pro-life prayer vigils and educational campaigns. Still others give powerful witness to the sanctity of life by working (professionally or as volun-teers) in hospices for persons dying of AIDS or other condi-tions. Counseling services like *Birthright* that assist women with problem pregnancies offer another outlet for pro-life commitment, as do *post*-abortion counseling services for women coping with the often traumatic effects of this deadly procedure.

This list could be extended. Catholics looking for specifics will do well to seek ideas and suggestions from the pro-life committee in their parish (not every parish has one of these, of course, but many do, and Monsignor Hellman, to his credit, has made sure that Holy Family does), or the pro-life office of their diocese. No community lacks opportunities for serving the cause of human life. Look around—you won't have to look far to find a way. Even (and perhaps especially) ordinary one-on-one conversations with family members and friends can provide important opportunities to testify to the sanctity of life.

3. PROMOTING FREEDOM OF CONSCIENCE AND RELIGIOUS FREEDOM

The Czech Dominican, in the United States for graduate studies, was telling me how he came to be expelled from the seminary.

It had happened several years earlier, under communism, at a time when religious orders weren't permitted to function openly in his country. Therefore, he was preparing for the priesthood in a diocesan seminary.

In an effort to placate the regime, the seminary officials had decided to mark a communist anniversary with a special ceremony. The idea of a communist celebration in his seminary struck my friend as being in poor taste, so he hid a picture of Our Lady of Fatima behind a Red banner. At a key moment during the event, he raised the banner, and—lo and behold—the Virgin Mary was center stage.

He was expelled.

In greater or lesser ways, millions of other people have suffered for their faith throughout much of the twentieth century. But that was before the nonviolent revolution of 1989, which brought about the fall of communism in Eastern Europe. Discrimination against religion and religious believers is a thing of the past… isn't it?

Sad to say, it isn't. Religious persecution and offenses against the consciences of believers are still occurring in many places. (Try being a Catholic loyal to the Holy See in China, or a Christian in the Sudan.) Even in the United States and countries like it, where religious liberty is a constitutionally guaranteed right, there are serious problems.

Obviously, in America religious believers needn't fear imprisonment and bloody martyrdom, nor even the sort of harassment my Czech friend experienced. But there is an insidious and powerful enemy of faith abroad in the land. Although it goes by various names (or even by none—it's often simply depicted as conventional wisdom, the body of mixed fact and fancy that "everybody knows" to be true), the generic name for it is secular humanism. It is an implacable foe of religion, committed to harrying faith out of the marketplace of ideas and imposing impotence on religion by requiring an extreme version of church-state separation which the Founding Fathers wouldn't recognize.

American Catholics and other people of faith should take very seriously the threat posed by secular humanism to religious liberty. As the Catholic writer George Weigel remarks, the country's "cultural elite"—those prominent in secular academia, in the media, and in popular entertainment—are "thoroughly secularized." And "here, at the chief cultural switchboards of American life, the consensus on the public role of religion is simple, direct, and propagated with great (some might say, fanatical) zeal: there is no place for religion in the public life of the American republic."[1] Sometimes this militantly secularistic worldview operates in visibly aggressive ways—for instance, court cases challenging expressions of religious belief in public life. But very often its activity is silent and unseen, like a kind of ideological poison gas.

Like many large cultural and social problems, this is one that isolated individuals may think they can do little or nothing about. Yet some people do have real opportunities to make a contribution on their own: I think of educators, people in communications media, politics, and law.

For other concerned religious believers, Catholics, other Christians, Jews, and Muslims alike, it can be important not to remain *isolated* but instead to join with others in protecting religious rights. We must protect not only the right to the private *practice* of religion but also the right to assert and defend a positive religious role in the shaping and conduct of public life. In the Catholic sphere, one group committed to doing this is the Catholic League for Religious and Civil Rights, a national organization with local chapters in several cities. (Information about the League and its work is available from its national office: 1011 First Avenue, New York, New York 10022.)

4. FOSTERING HEALTHY MARRIAGES AND FAMILIES

Suppose a Catholic wife and husband take seriously the duties sketched for them in Canon 226—to contribute to "the upbuilding of the people of God" through marriage and family life and to provide for the Christian upbringing of their children. They've got a problem on their hands! Not only do they receive little or no encouragement from the surrounding secular culture, time and time again they will find serious roadblocks thrown in their way by that secular culture as it labors blindly and self-destructively to make certain they don't succeed. And let's face it, sometimes they won't receive much support from their parishes and other institutions and programs in the Church.

The evidence is overwhelming: legalized abortion, a highly permissive and hedonistic view of sex, consumerism, "no-fault" divorce, a skeptical and scornful attitude toward traditional morality, the doctrinaire exclusion of religion from public schools and other public institutions, propaganda declaring cohabitation and homosexuality to be legitimate "alternative life styles." All these things (and a lot more it's too depressing to name) are routinely promoted by the media and defended by supposedly responsible public servants as matters of public policy. Living up to the demands of Christian marriage and family life has never been easy. Today there are times when it can seem nearly impossible.

The obvious conclusion is that married couples willing to make the effort deserve lots of help. One of the best sources of such help lies in close, friendly association with other couples who share the same problems and the same ideals.

Let me offer a little personal testimony on that.

For many years now, my wife and I have been members of a Catholic couples' group called Teams of Our Lady. It is of French origin ("team" is "équipe" in French, and it probably comes across better in that language than in English). An individual team is made up of four or five or six couples, with a priest as chaplain. They meet monthly, rotating among one anothers' homes, for a meal, some prayer, and conversation.

In between, the individual couples try to observe a few simple religious practices in the home. They also try to enhance their shared communication. And, of course, their friends in the team are available, to a greater or lesser degree, for consultation and just plain schmoozing, as need and circumstances dictate.

The basic idea underlying this simple program is to foster something called "conjugal spirituality"—the special way to sanctity for persons whose vocation calls them to the married state. What the team concept adds is the encouragement, support, and reinforcement of Christian friends who also know marriage and family life from the inside, who experience the same joys and defeats, successes and frustrations, and whose faith sharing and perseverance are a reminder to the individual couple that they're not alone in their struggle to live up to the ideal of Christian marriage in the midst of a neo-pagan world.

My point isn't that everyone has to join the Teams of Our Lady (but if you're interested, you can get information from Teams of Our Lady, Holy Childhood Parish Building, 140 W. Main Street, Floor 3, Harbor Springs, Michigan 49740). Many people have found this particular group helpful, but there are other groups and movements more or less committed to the same thing. Indeed, there's no absolute reason why a couple has to join anything, especially if they are not joiners or they cannot find some organized group or movement where they live.

For many people, nevertheless, it will at least prove helpful to form bonds with other couples who share the same religious faith and moral values and are struggling to make them living realities. Having identified a few such people in your parish or neighborhood, start meeting regularly (monthly is probably about right) to talk about your experience in the great adventure called "Christian marriage." Invite a congenial priest to join you if there's one available. A potluck supper and a little wine may help the conversation flow. It may also be useful to have some designated reading material to discuss. The gospel for that day is good for the purpose, but it doesn't have to be that.

Don't look for quick results and dramatic payoffs. Forming and sustaining this kind of informal community with other Christian couples is not a problem-solver for troubled marriages (that may require professional help), nor is it a hedge against the strains that come with raising kids, sickness in the family, financial problems, and all the rest.

Over time, though, it is an answer—the best available, it seems to me—to the debilitating sense of isolation that today's hostile secular culture otherwise is likely to create in individual couples struggling to turn the ideal of Christian matrimony into the reality of a flesh-and-blood Catholic marriage and to hand on faith to their children. It is also the best and arguably the only way that such people can respond to the breathtaking challenge set before them by Pope John Paul: that they—not somebody else, but they—become "the primary social nucleus" from which the healing and renewal of our sick secular society in time will come.

5. PARTICIPATION IN THE WORKS OF CHARITY

There is an ongoing debate in America about the relative roles of government and the private sector in responding to human needs. It's an interesting and important question, and one about which most of us have opinions. I surely do.

But beyond noting that, pretty clearly, government and the private sector both have roles to play, I am not going to argue any particular side of the question here. Instead I want to call attention to something else. Whatever the correct balance between public and private sector may actually be, it's important that individuals and the private groups in which they participate be active. Leaving everything to public institutions and the sometimes frayed social safety net is a mistake that sooner or later leads to the "all-too-easy and generalized disengagement from a sense of duty" of which the Pope also speaks.

There are many reasons for saying that, but one is particularly pertinent here. To quote Pope John Paul again: "Charity towards one's neighbor... represents the most immediate, ordinary and habitual way that leads to the Christian animation of the temporal order, the specific duty of the lay faithful" (*Christifideles Laici*, 41). Sections of the Code of Canon Law express the same idea in various ways. For example, Canon 222.2, speaks of the duty of Christians to promote social justice and to "assist the poor from their own resources"—with "resources" most assuredly not limited only to paying taxes and contributing money to the Church.

Material poverty is the most obvious way of being poor, but

it is not the only way. Many groups and persons in our society suffer the poverty of cultural, emotional, and spiritual deprivation. And just as there are many kinds of poverty, so there are many ways of responding. In very general terms, these fall into two large categories: individual initiative and organized, group activity. Both are necessary. No one need look far to find a way of getting involved.

The Church herself sponsors numerous movements and institutions that respond to human needs. The St. Vincent de Paul Society has a long and honorable record of service in this field. The Knights of Columbus and other Catholic organizations are notable embodiments of volunteerism in action. But if what already exists doesn't suit your taste, Canon 215 points to the right of members of the Church "freely to found and to govern associations for charitable and religious purposes." As to the areas of need: hospitals, retirement homes, hospices, shelters for the homeless and for battered women, feeding programs for the poor and shut-ins, sports and tutoring for youth, and home visiting for the elderly—all these and many other programs have constant needs for helping hands.

But service to the neighbor in need also takes in lots besides working in a soup kitchen or bundling up old clothes or working as a candy-striper. Professionals like doctors and attorneys have many opportunities for *pro bono* work on behalf of needy patients and clients. People with the necessary skills and expertise can do useful advocacy and education. My wife belongs to a group which cheers up old folks in nursing homes by bringing pets to visit them. Does it work? You bet it does!

If you're looking for suggestions, contact your parish social concerns committee or diocesan Catholic charities and see what's available. Phone the volunteers office at a nearby hospital or retirement home. Ask around. There is, to repeat, no shortage of things that need doing.

Don't overlook the areas of need—the people who need helping—right around you. Here, especially, generous individuals can accomplish a great deal on their own. There's the woman up the street with early Alzheimer's who has to be driven to the grocery store and the doctor. In the next block, there's the mother with two young children who needs an afternoon off from child care now and then. There's also the retired widower in the apartment upstairs who seems to have no family or friends.

For most people, of course, giving money is an obvious way of participating in the works of charity. Canon 222.1 speaks of the duty to contribute to the Church for that purpose. It shouldn't be neglected. But neither should giving money be a substitute for personal involvement on the part of those who can manage it. It isn't just those in obvious need whom we help this way—it is ourselves.

6. TAKING PART IN POLITICS AND PUBLIC LIFE

"Who, me—run for office? You've got to be kidding!"

Not necessarily. Listen to what the pope says: "Charges of careerism, idolatry of power, egoism, and corruption that are sometimes directed at persons in government, parliaments, the ruling classes, or political parties, as well as the common opinion that participating in politics is an absolute moral danger, does not in the least justify either skepticism or the absence of Christians from public life" (*Christifideles Laici*, 42). If good people don't establish the tone and set the course of politics and public life, bad people certainly will.

Generally speaking, we get the kind of political leadership we deserve. You say you aren't pleased with the face of politics lately—all those "personally opposed" pro-abortion politicians, office-holders under the thumb of special interests, takers of payoffs and recipients of borderline-legal perks, hacks whose chief preoccupation is getting re-elected, and other public figures of similarly dubious ethics who offend you? Don't be too quick to blame somebody else. Your own passivity and refusal to get involved in politics may be helping to put such people in their positions of power and keep them there.

To be sure, not everyone has the talent, training, and temperament to be a successful politician, although undoubtedly the personal vocations of some direct them that way. But many more people could—and should—be active in politics and public affairs at all levels than now are. A lot of political activity is open to anyone willing to make the necessary investment of time and effort. Consider attending and taking part in meetings of public bodies where citizen participation is welcome, writing thoughtful and well-informed letters to elected officials as well as the media, getting involved in the grassroots activities of political parties with an eye to influencing their policies for the better, or working for deserving candidates for office. None of this is glamorous, but cumulatively it is very important.

And, of course, there is voting. Some people seldom or never vote, while others vote on the basis of what must candidly be called selfish or frivolous considerations. I know a woman who voted for a particular candidate because she liked the pictures she'd seen of his cat. That may have been a reason to vote for the cat, but certainly not for the man.

Conscientious voting is an expression of the virtue of patriotism—that love of one's country or community which itself is a form of love of neighbor. Note, though, that voting should be conscientious and informed. That takes effort: keeping up with the issues, learning candidates' views and other qualifications, resisting the over-simplifications and appeals to prejudice and passion typical of political campaigns.

For Catholics, it also requires that issues and candidates be judged in light of the Church's teaching. Members of the Church are free to make up their own minds on political questions. Vatican Council II points out that the Church herself is "not bound by ties to any political system." Yet the Church's doctrine does shed the gospel's light on countless public issues.

The notion that religion has nothing to say to and about politics is simply false.

Canon 227 calls attention to both sides of this particular coin—the freedom of the laity with regard to temporal affairs, including politics, and their duty to be guided by Catholic moral values. Next time, dear lady—vote for the candidate, not the cat.

7. PLACING THE INDIVIDUAL AT THE CENTER OF SOCIO-ECONOMIC LIFE

Some time ago I took part in a television discussion with a man who'd written a book about corporate responsibility. Something he said stuck in my mind:

"The basic purpose of a corporation is to make money. No doubt a corporation which treats its employees well, doesn't pollute the environment, and deals fairly with consumers will generally be more successful than one which fails in these matters. Still, the fundamental reason why a corporation exists is to make money, not any or all of those good things."

Possibly a lot of people would agree. Yet this view of corporations and their relationship to morality is at odds with Catholic social doctrine. Other things being equal, corporations and commercial enterprises of all kinds should make money. Many benefits, to society and to individuals, flow from that. But ultimately the central reason for the existence of corporations and businesses and social institutions of all kinds lies elsewhere.

Where? In the individual human person. Finally, all social structures and institutions, including those of a profit-making nature, either exist for the sake of human flourishing or they are radically flawed—evil—not only in their controlling vision but, quite possibly, in the way they operate as well.

Back in the nineteenth century Karl Marx concluded that, in

the aftermath of the Industrial Revolution, workers had become "alienated" from their work. Communism may be a spent force today, but this problem of worker alienation lingers. "There is no lack of willing workers in America," remarks a contemporary observer of the American social scene, Christopher Lasch of the University of Rochester. "What is missing is the kind of work that confers dignity and self-respect, a sense of vocation. Without that, work becomes a means to something else—wealth, social status, or sheer survival."[2]

The result is apparent in two views of work that seem to be pretty widely held these days. One is the attitude summed up by saying, "I'll only do what I must to get by"; the other is, "I'll do whatever it takes to succeed." The first breeds carelessness and slipshod work and the feeling that work is essentially a painful, meaningless grind. The second is the breeding ground for workaholism, cut-throat competition, and some forms of white collar crime.

The root cause of these social plagues lies in the way much work is structured—in other words, in the nature of many jobs themselves. Efforts to defend workers' rights stress wages and benefits, hours and working conditions. These things are enormously important. Yet relatively little attention is given to a matter of equal importance, namely, the actual work to be done. The goal should be to ensure that real-life jobs offer people adequate opportunities for personal fulfillment through worthwhile activity in the service of the common good.

Pope John Paul commends the ideal of work carried on "with professional competence [and] with human honesty." That will mean different things for owners and managers on the one hand and employees on the other. In concrete terms, "professional competence" and "human honesty" take different forms for different kinds of workers (professionals, blue-collar workers, persons engaged in service occupations, farm workers, and others).

It would be foolish to imply that the problem of alienation

from work has an easy solution. There are such things as meaningless, dead-end jobs. What can anybody do about that?

I shall return to the subject of work in discussing lay spirituality near the end of this book. In that context—spirituality—there are some special points to be made about work. Here I only want to point to one of the major challenges facing Christians and other people of good will in the workplace today. In whatever ways are available to them, they need to press responsibly for a restructuring of work—of jobs themselves—so that, as much as is humanly possible, the work that people do will contribute to their own human growth and to the fulfillment of those for whom they do it.

Call this the humanizing of work. It is an apostolate of immense importance. And the fact that the need to humanize work generally is not recognized only makes the need that much more urgent.

8. EVANGELIZING CULTURE

Ideas are important. Pope John Paul speaks of the "privileged places of culture"—education, the sciences and technology, arts and humanities. It is here that attitudes are formed and the future course of society is set. In particular, he says, "the privileged way at present" is found in the communication media.

And here, too, there are major challenges for the Catholic laity.

A while back, I attended an invitation-only gathering whose theme was media coverage of family issues. Professional journalists and specialists in several fields had assembled to exchange views. At one session an economist noted that Americans who belong to intact two-parent families are, generally speaking, financially better off than those in "nontraditional" groupings (single-parent families and the like).

The poverty rate among the latter is four times higher than among the former.

Even so, the speaker noted, the number of Americans in the non-traditional situations is rising rapidly. Why is that? He speculated that it has to do with social acceptance of alternative lifestyles and that this development itself was a product of moral relativism.

Pretty unexceptionable stuff, many people would say. But a writer who covers family issues for a major American daily newspaper bridled at this analysis. She was, she said, the child of divorced parents, she'd been living with a man for five years, and she didn't consider herself any worse off than anybody else. As for alternative lifestyles, she posed the textbook question of a moral relativist: "Who am I to judge?"

A unique case? Not at all. Social science research has shown that the journalists who staff American media are more socially liberal, much less religious, and much more morally permissive than most other Americans. Does it make a difference? Journalists sometimes deny that it does, but other studies point to a different conclusion: the liberal bias of the media elite colors the picture of the world that they depict for the rest of us.

The problem by no means is limited to journalism. It also exists in so-called "entertainment" media. A movie nominated for six Academy Awards not long ago was described by veteran film critic John Simon as "homosexual propaganda." Pro-homosexual works routinely appear on Broadway and receive critical acclaim. Students of the entertainment industry say some of the most influential figures in the "show business community," promote single parenthood and out-of-wedlock birth as a matter of conviction.

It would be comforting to think that religiously committed people could turn things around simply by pursuing careers in media. No doubt they should do that, but the problem won't be solved that easily. Social scientist Stanley Rothman, who has studied the situation professionally, writes that journalists and other "cultural elites" are at the cutting edge of a revolution transforming America: "This revolution involves indifference (and sometimes hostility) toward many traditional institutions, including religious institutions."[3]

Besides seeking careers in secular media, then, Catholics and other religiously motivated people who grasp the impact that media have on cultural values need to busy themselves with creating and strengthening *alternative* media—newspapers and periodicals, publishing houses, film and broadcasting production centers and networks—where Judeo-Christian values can get a fair shake. Those not personally involved in media work can do their part by supporting such alternative media—and by *not* supporting commercial secular media that manifest overt hostility to religion and religious values, as some now regularly do.

In many ways, the task of "evangelizing culture" has today become a war of ideas. Unless Catholic laypeople become actively engaged in this fight, it's a battle that faith could lose.

That may seem like a sour note on which to end a discussion of how the laity can exercise their rights and satisfy their responsibilities to—in the words of canon law—"imbue the order of temporal affairs with the spirit of the gospel" (Canon 225.2). I don't mean to end on a downer. But it serves no useful purpose to approach this subject in the spirit of Pollyanna and pretend that the task facing us is an easy one. In fact, it promises to be very difficult.

To some extent, of course, the world and the Church have always been more or less in conflict. Speaking of the *unredeemed* world, Jesus said it would be so: "If the world hates you, know that it has hated me before it hated you.... If they persecuted me, they will persecute you" (Jn 15:18-20). Since the rationalistic and ultimately antireligious Enlightenment of the seventeenth and eighteenth centuries, secular society has moved away from religion and moral values at an accelerating pace. The terrible results have become tragically apparent throughout much of the twentieth century. The reign of secular humanism has been disastrous for the world, whether Marxist and messianic in those unhappy countries where communism held or still holds sway or self-absorbed and pleasure-seeking in its Western "consumerist" guise.

Under the leadership of Pope John XXIII and Pope Paul VI, the Second Vatican Council sought to renew the Church so that she would be able to close the gap between herself and the world. In this way, Christians would place the gospel of Jesus Christ fully at the service of contemporary men and women. That effort continues under Pope John Paul II.

It is not just some abstract entity called "the world" about which, ultimately, the Church is concerned. Like Jesus, she is interested in human beings—both their temporal welfare and their eternal welfare (not set apart in separate, watertight compartments either, but understood as being directly, intimately related to each other). Her members must share this concern. "The joys and the hopes, the griefs and the anxieties of the men of this age, especially those who are poor or in any way afflicted, these too are the joys and hopes, the griefs and anxieties of the followers of Christ," Vatican Council II declared (*Gaudium et Spes*, 1).

The primary agents of the great and noble program implied in those words are Catholic laypeople. The laity are not the long arm of the bishops, controlled and directed by the clerical hierarchy (as both the clericalist view of things and anti-Catholic critics of the Church seem to imagine). Rather, Catholic laypeople are autonomous, self-reliant Christians who have their own special share of responsibility for the mission of the Church, their own proper work to do on behalf of God's kingdom.

Consciously, at least, the secular world isn't waiting eagerly to hear the gospel of Christ preached to it. On the contrary, the world usually can be counted on to respond to the Jesus' good news with indifference, contempt and hostility, and with persecution for those who proclaim it. Some will listen and respond positively. Many will not. The apostolate in and to the secular order can involve carrying the cross of Christ. That, perhaps, is the highest right and duty of the laity.

NINE

Four Special Problems

YOUR RIGHT IS MY RESPONSIBILITY. At a minimum, I'm obliged not to step on your toes, either literally or metaphorically. And vice versa—don't you step on mine.

Understanding the relationship between duties and rights, and between those who possess them, is essential to an accurate grasp of our subject. Troubles arise when people overlook the link between duty and right or rebel against it. This can happen when, for example, I deny that you have a certain right you claim (and so, of course, reject the suggestion that I have some obligation in regard to it), or you acknowledge that I really do have a certain right, yet choose to violate it just the same.

All of this is just as true in the Church as it is any place else. For even though the Church is a communion of human beings rooted in communion with God, her essential *human* element carries with it all the limitations and faults common to our fallen race. That is by way of making a painfully obvious point: conflicts concerning rights and responsibilities occur among

175

the members of the ecclesial community too.

One way in which, typically, this happens is for some person or persons in a position of authority to exceed the limits of their authority and demand things of subordinates that oughtn't to be demanded. Another way, also common, is for subordinates to resist the reasonable requirements of those in authority. And, of course, two or more parties, none of whom is an "authority," can come into conflict over questions of duty and right. People in all settings, not just the Church, are prone to act this way. In the *Church*, however, such behavior has a special dimension, since the parties to conflicts are especially likely to appeal to religious ideals and moral principles as the bases for their claims and counter-claims.

In the Catholic Church today, the spirit of religious authoritarianism is less visibly at work than in former times, but it still exists. Consider, for instance, the pastor who decides to remodel the parish church at considerable expense in order to suit his notions of current liturgical style, without discussing the project in advance with the parishioners. He also expects the people to foot the bill—and then complains when they're reluctant to do so. Or consider the lay principal of a Catholic school who makes an arbitrary change in the school uniform without consulting the parents who have to pay for the new clothes. Consider as well the individual cleric (acting on his own whim) or the entire episcopal conference (acting on the advice of "experts" or at the urging of interest groups) engaged in making changes in the liturgy unsought by ordinary Catholics. Who can doubt that such things happen?

As noted, though, people in authority are by no means the only offenders. The legitimate directives of those in authority often are ignored or resisted by those who have a duty to obey. This reaches very far. How many Catholics today rationalize their rejection of Catholic doctrine and discipline by railing against the Polish pope? (The implication is that John Paul II's ethnic background renders him incapable of understanding the presumably more enlightened views of American or Western European Catholics.) How many appeal to individual conscience, or even in some cases to a special charism alleged to have been bestowed on them directly by God, in order to excuse their refusal to accept the authority of the Church in which they claim membership? The answer is: Quite a few. There also are many cases in which people with some fancied grievance against authority have opted to "go public" with their complaints, defaming those they disagree with and exploiting the Christian reluctance of those in authority to respond in kind.

On the other hand, it should not be supposed that somebody is always clearly at fault when conflicts occur in the Church. Situations not infrequently arise in which rights and duties are *not* very clear, and sincere persons who want to do the right thing can sincerely disagree about what that is.

Canon law offers principles for attempting to resolve such disputes—as well as disputes in which someone is clearly at fault—but by no means is it a panacea for them all. In fact, the Church's law does not provide a well-developed judicial system for settling conflicts.

As we have seen, while the 1983 code was under development, some canonists argued for the inclusion of administrative tribunals for this purpose, but such tribunals are nowhere to be found in the finished code. And, as we have further seen, that may be just as well right now: in these times of conflict and polarization, the community of faith would hardly gain in unity from what could appear to be a legally sanctioned invitation to Catholics in conflict to haul one another into an ecclesiastical court.

It's often been said that this is a litigious age—that individuals and groups are very quick to have recourse to the law in order to vindicate their rights (or what they claim as rights). That may be a good thing in some ways. But unquestionably it has raised the level of tension within civil society, while also inviting activist lawyers and judges to set the course of law and public policy on tracks more congenial to their own ideological preferences than to the common good of all. No responsible Catholic should want to see the Church go the same way.

So what good is canon law for conflict resolution? The answer concerns the vision of the Church—the ecclesiology of communion—that is embodied in the code. This way of understanding the Church doesn't offer neat, clear answers to every problem. But it does provide a way of *thinking* about relationships in the Church that can lead to answers and solutions among Catholics of genuine (not feigned) good will.

Against that general background, I want to discuss four particular problems—four conflict areas—in the life of the Catholic Church today. These have to do with: 1) public opinion; 2) parents' rights in education; 3) women's concerns, including the ordination of women as priests; and 4) parish renewal. What I have to say will not solve any problems, but it may suggest where solutions can be found.

1. PUBLIC OPINION IN THE CHURCH

Canon 212.3 says Catholics have a right and "even at times a duty" to tell the leaders of the Church what they think about matters pertaining to her welfare, as well as a right to share their opinions with one another.

Any healthy society needs public opinion. There are several reasons for that. By expressing themselves in a systematic, orderly way, people let off steam and enjoy the feeling that they matter. Public opinion brings good ideas and practical suggestions to the attention of decision-makers. It contributes to an atmosphere of mutual respect and collaboration that makes it easier for all involved to work together in solving common problems and facing common challenges.

In the Church, public opinion is important not only for

pragmatic reasons like these—essentially, because things work better that way—but also, at a deeper level, because allowing public opinion to play a recognized, respected role expresses the Church's own special nature as *communio*: that is, a communion of persons who are essentially equal in dignity as Christians and who share responsibility for the same Christian mission to the world, according to their individual ecclesial roles and their personal circumstances.

"That's all good and fine," someone might say, "but there's a problem. Vatican Council II speaks of 'agencies set up by the Church' in and through which laypeople can tell their pastors what's on their mind. But the Council doesn't say what these 'agencies' are and it is by no means clear where to find them in the Church today.

"Leave aside griping and backbiting—I grant that those things aren't 'public opinion' as we're speaking of it here. But suppose that you as a conscientious Catholic layperson have given serious thought to something you consider a real problem (the absence from most homilies of adult-level catechetical instruction, say) and now you want to respectfully share your conclusions with the bishop. What are you supposed to do? How can you even get his attention?"

That's a very good question. One obvious answer is to write the bishop a letter. Bishops do, in fact, receive many letters of this sort from laypeople in their dioceses. Yet many other letters never get written or sent, for a variety of reasons. As far as many Catholics can tell, their bishop has no interest whatsoever in hearing from them about anything at all. They've never been told anything different, and the lack of encouragement is a considerable disincentive to write. Others simply have no idea where to reach the bishop. Look in the telephone directory? That sounds like trying to call city hall.

But suppose someone does get a letter written and mailed: then what? In due course he or she may receive a response that looks suspiciously like a form letter: "Thanks very much." Did the bishop or anybody else pay any real attention? Did the bishop himself even read the letter? Chances are the individual will never know. (I pass over in silence those cases in which the response is a rebuke to the lay person who's had the nerve to tell a bishop—or someone else in authority in the Church— something he didn't care to hear.)

I don't mean to suggest that everyone who writes his or her bishop, or thinks of writing, has a valid point to make. There's at least as much crank mail in circulation in the Church as any-where else. I am only saying that, as a matter of fact, ordinary Catholics who wish to share their thoughts with Church leader-ship can be pardoned for feeling they've run into a brick wall. Often, the "agencies" of public opinion about which the Coun-cil speaks don't seem to exist. Even where they do—in the form of parish and diocesan pastoral councils, for example—they often appear to be more or less ineffectual. Elsewhere, strong-willed pastoral leaders like Monsignor Hellman have simply stonewalled pressures to create such bodies, believing that they know as much as is necessary about the state of public opinion.

In fairness, of course, it should be recognized that the American bishops have made consultation of various kinds a part of their operating procedure at the national level for some years now. While the bishops (like every other leadership group one can think of) certainly are capable of surprising lapses back into secrecy and arbitrary procedures, regional and diocesan "hearings" and consultations by mail nevertheless have been part of the process by which several major episcopal documents have been prepared.

That marks a big change from the past, when bishops' state-ments usually were prepared in secret, with the involvement of a handful of clerical advisors, and were kept under wraps until the bishops chose to release them. Episcopal documents these days may or may not be better than they used to be, but the process by which some of them get written is surely more open.

Yet somehow ordinary folks don't seem to be part of it. The

bishops' consultations of which I speak seem to have an elitist slant. Activists and interest groups are involved; the women and men in the pew usually aren't. There also seems to be a strange principle of selectivity involved regarding subject matter. Has anyone in authority asked lay Catholics how they feel, for instance, about "inclusive language" in the liturgy? My congratulations to those who can say yes. No one has ever asked me.

The authorities might say several things in reply.

1. Ordinary lay Catholics don't know enough about many matters of concern to the Church to have anything useful to say about them. The answer to that comes in three parts. First, to the extent that the observation is true, it points to an enormous need for education—catechesis, as it is technically called—at all levels in the Church. Second, how can you be sure if you don't ask? Third, the central reason for encouraging and attending to the expression of public opinion in the Church is not to collect good ideas—although good ideas certainly ought to be welcome—but simply to let people exercise their right to speak their minds.

2. Whenever laypeople are asked for their input, only a few respond. No doubt. Probably it's that way in every group and always will be. Still, in the Catholic context, the fact is that laypeople are just not used to being asked what they think and are caught by surprise when it happens. There is a lot of deeply ingrained apathy and indifference to be overcome. Keep at it. It is going to take time to break down the negative attitudes and bad habits formed by a tradition of noninvolvement arising from clericalism. But once people get used to the idea that those in authority really do care what they think, some of them are likely to start thinking more.

3. I have a pastoral council in my parish or diocese, along

with any number of other different committees and advisory groups. Laypeople serve on many of these. Surely that's enough? That depends. In fact, such bodies have the capacity of being the "agencies" of public opinion of which Vatican Council II speaks. Note that the Code of Canon Law provides for pastoral councils, and for finance councils with lay members, at the parish and diocesan levels: for example, canons 228, 492, 511-514, 537.

But for these bodies really to be instruments of a healthy public opinion, they must think of themselves as such and operate that way. Too many consultative groups in the Church have become the preserve of a comparative handful of people, so that, from the outside at least, they resemble self-perpetuating "in" groups. It is no solution to the problem of public opinion in the Church to limit participation in councils and committees and the like to the relatively small number of laypeople, well-motivated as they are, who naturally gravitate to them because of their clericalized interests, or whom the clergy in charge choose to invite to participate because they're "safe." In certain places, too, it's an open secret that lay Catholics who are both articulate and orthodox stand little chance of being allowed into the consultative process. That, it seems, is a privilege reserved for those who are predictably liberal.

But the need now, I believe, is not so much for new structures and processes of consultation (especially if the "new" were to turn out to be as inward-looking and elitist as some of those that already exist) as it is for changes in attitude. We need changes in how members of the Church think of one another and of the Church herself. In dealing with this issue, it may be that the first and most important thing to do is to fix clearly in our minds the answer to a fundamental question: Why should the pastoral leaders of the Church seek to find out what her other members—for the most part, laypeople—have to say?

John Henry Newman got to the heart of the matter at the end of a classic essay written in 1859. There he quotes a contemporary account of the rejoicing with which laypeople in the fifth century greeted the news that the ecumenical Council of Ephesus, responding to a heresy of that day, had affirmed the doctrine that the Blessed Virgin Mary is the Mother of God. The future cardinal then commented:

"I think certainly that the *Ecclesia docens* [the teaching Church] is more happy when she has such enthusiastic partisans about her as are here represented, than when she cuts off the faithful from the study of her divine doctrines and the sympathy of her divine contemplations, and requires from them a *fides implicita* [implicit faith] in her word, which in the educated classes will terminate in indifference, and in the poorer in superstition."[1]

Newman wasn't saying that bishops and popes should consult laypeople to find out what they ought to teach. Nor was he saying that (as defenders of theological dissent today sometimes seem to suggest) doctrine must be changed to suit the shifting tides of public opinion. Rather, Newman's point was that in matters pertaining to faith, laypeople can testify to the faith of the Church. Further, where practical policies are concerned (raising and spending money, opening and closing schools, parishes, and other institutions, launching and terminating programs of many different kinds), laypeople who are well-informed and well-motivated often have good advice to give. Encouraging public opinion in the Church may involve difficulties, but in the long run the difficulties are a lot worse where there is no public opinion.

One more quote from Vatican II (the *Constitution on the Church*) is pertinent here:

A great many benefits are to be hoped for from this familiar dialogue between the laity and their pastors: in the laity, a strengthened sense of personal responsibility, a renewed enthusiasm, a more ready application of their talents to the projects of their pastors. The latter, for their part, aided by the experience of the laity, can more clearly and more suitably come to decisions regarding spiritual and temporal matters. In this way, the whole Church, strengthened by each one of its members, can more effectively fulfill its mission for the life of the world. *Lumen Gentium*, 37

That's a text worth meditating on.

2. PARENTAL RIGHTS IN EDUCATION

Suppose you're a conscientious Catholic mother and your daughter Margaret Mary is a sixth-grader in Holy Family School. One day she comes home and announces that sex education classes start next week. She shows you the text to be used, and, even though it could be lots worse, you think it also could be a lot better.

Furthermore, you've always believed that education in human sexuality is essentially the parents' responsibility. Isn't that what the Church herself says officially whenever the subject comes up? Consistent with that, you've tried to fulfill your responsibility with Margaret Mary, beginning her gradual introduction to the facts of life and their Christian meaning when she was quite small and continuing it all along the line in ways suited to her age and developmental level. In fact, you think you've been doing a pretty good job.

So you make an appointment to see the principal. It's not a happy meeting.

You appreciate the importance of education in human sexuality, you explain to Sister Alice, and you're glad the school shares your concern. However, you regard education in human sexuality as something for you to handle—doesn't the Church say as much? And you *have* been handling it, quite well thank you, for some time. Moreover, to tell the truth, that text which Margaret Mary brought home doesn't look entirely satisfactory to you. In view of all that, can your daughter be excused?

Sister Alice is pleasant but firm. Margaret Mary is a wonderful little girl, and it's also wonderful to find a mother as concerned about her daughter's education as you are. Many parents neglect to teach their children a Christian view of sexuality. But the children are learning *something* anyway—from television, from their peers, from secular culture generally. The school would be remiss if it failed to step in. *And...* the faculty has worked very hard at planning and implementing this program, the curriculum and the teaching materials have the approval of the diocesan education office, it would be embarrassing to Margaret Mary and disruptive to the class to excuse her. *The answer is no.* (What Sister leaves unsaid, but what seems clear anyway, is that if you don't like it, you can find another school.)

What's a parent to do?

No point appealing to Monsignor Hellman. He stays out of school affairs, and he'd back up Sister Alice anyway. (If he got the principal sufficiently miffed, her order might even pull out of Holy Family—there aren't enough nuns any more to meet all the requests for their services, so why should they stay where they aren't appreciated?) The bishop? At most, he might check out your complaint with the Monsignor, but he probably wouldn't do even that. He doesn't care to offend his senior pastors (who can blame him for that?). Anyway his own education office approved the program you want your daughter excused from. You *could* start shopping for another school, but Margaret Mary would be upset—and who can say a new school would be better? So you simmer down, with a nagging question in the back of your head: Whatever happened to parents' rights?

Canon 226.2 affirms the right and the duty of parents to educate. Parents, it says, are "especially to care for the Christian education of their children according to the teaching handed on by the Church." Nothing new about that. Time and again the Church has taught that parents are the primary educators of their children. A commentary on the 1983 code cited earlier, says it contains "a veritable bill of parental rights and obligations" scattered throughout.

The hierarchical Church also has grave obligations in Christian education. This is among the most solemn duties of bishops and pastors. (See, for instance, canons 773-780 on catechetical instruction and canons 796-806 on Catholic schools.) They respond in various ways, including providing schools and other formal programs. Generally speaking, parents who patronize the Church's programs are grateful for their existence, and have good reason to be.

Yet even where all the adult parties to the educational enterprise—pastors, administrators, teachers, and parents—are conscientious people trying to do their duty, conflicts can arise. The example above illustrates that. Admittedly, I set it up in a way suggesting that the parent was in the right. Tell the same story from the principal's point of view, and it could look different (nervous and over-protective mother, too quick to try to yank her daughter out of something that could be to her advantage, and so on.).

Once again, we face a basic question: In conflict situations in the Church, how can the conflicts be resolved? And once more that forces us to face a basic fact: There is no mechanism—no system, no established procedure—for resolving them. Catholics must work out their differences for themselves (or else fail to work them out), with little besides their good sense and good will to guide them.

Here, nevertheless, are some thoughts which could be helpful in such efforts where the issue revolves around the parental right to educate.

To begin with, it seems clear that ordinarily a certain preference or priority should be given to that right. The strong assumption should be in favor of the parental role, especially when parents make it clear that they wish to exercise it in the face of someone else's conflicting ideas of what is best for their children.

This parental primacy is a truism in the psychological order. Everybody knows that, for good or for ill, what parents do or fail to do makes the first and most lasting impression on their offspring. Even so, there is a tendency in some quarters today to suppose that somebody or something else—society, the state, perhaps even the Church—*gives* parents such educational rights as they possess, and that the same source is entitled to withhold or withdraw parental rights when it cares to. Instead of the school working for the parents, it's the other way around.

"Since parents have conferred life on their children," Vatican II teaches, "they have a most solemn obligation to educate their offspring. Hence, parents must be acknowledged as the first and foremost educators of their children" (*Gravissimum Educationis,* 3).

There are several interesting things about that.

The Council starts with the idea of obligation instead of right. This is not moralism but clear thinking: as we have seen, duties undergird rights. No less important is the Council's linkage of *education* to the *begetting* of children. As Germain Grisez points out, "To be a father, to be a mother is more than physical reproduction. The parent not only must give the beginnings of physiological life, but must give all the beginnings.... Education is the psychic and spiritual equivalent of conception."[2]

Schools and other educational programs help parents to fulfill their sacred trust. That is crucial. Formal institutions and programs of education, including those provided by the Church, are parents' *helpers,* not their replacements.

Church teaching recognizes and affirms this fact. But real-life practice is significantly different. In the last three decades parents with reasonable grounds for questioning the adequacy or orthodoxy of Church-sponsored education sometimes have been patronized and dismissed by teachers, administrators, and religious authorities. Clericalism is one explanation for that.

The professionalization of Catholic education is another. It's a welcome development in principle, but it is at risk of being abused when experts automatically are thought to know more than parents about how and what their children should be taught.

Not to put all the blame on the educators and the authorities, though: some parents undoubtedly are overly suspicious and more or less closed-minded. Even more of a problem, as teachers and school administrators know well, is parental indifference—the attitude of parents who really don't care *what* happens in the classroom, as long as they don't have to get involved. (Speaking of sex education, I know a parochial school that carefully and consultatively instituted a responsible Christian program of education in human sexuality for children in three grades, then called a parents' week-night meeting to discuss the results. Six showed up.)

Another provision of canon law points the way out of this impasse. Canon 796.2 declares: "It is incumbent upon parents to cooperate closely with the [Catholic] school teachers to whom they entrust their children... in fulfilling their duty teachers are to collaborate closely with parents who are to be willingly heard and for whom associations or meetings are to be inaugurated and held in great esteem."

As is often the case, so here also the Church's law can tell us how things *ought* to be. Ongoing parent-teacher collaboration through associations established and operated for this purpose is the answer. It is up to us—all of us together—to see to it that that is how things really are. The Home and School Association of Holy Family Parish and its equivalents in thousands of other parishes have their work cut out for them.

3. WOMEN'S CONCERNS

Let's get down to cases at the start: Some women want to be ordained as priests. Unless and until that happens, they and those who agree with them will be convinced that the "patriar-chal" Church is denying Catholic women their rights. As they see it, furthermore, the problem goes deeper than the refusal to ordain women, neuralgic though that be. Denying women ordination, they contend, is the tip of the iceberg of a system of patriarchal oppression deforming the Catholic Church from top to bottom. The cause of women's rights in the Church demands that this system be smashed. There certainly are women in Holy Family, as everywhere else in the Church today, for whom these are articles of faith.

It isn't my intention here to enter into a full-scale discussion of the women's ordination question. In case anyone wonders, though, I agree with the position of the Church: that is, women cannot be ordained as priests.

It is not a matter of man-made law (I use the term advisedly) or social custom. Rather, it reflects the will of Christ. Evidence for that lies in the fact that, although Jesus was close to many women and counted them among his most cherished follow-ers, he called only men as apostles. It lies also in the Church's unbroken tradition testifying to what has been entrusted to her and preserved under the guidance of the Holy Spirit. As to why women cannot be ordained, the answer has nothing to do with gender-based inferiority or inequality. Instead it concerns what is sometimes called the "sacramental principle." Pre-eminently in the Eucharist, priests act *in persona Christi*—in the person of Christ. In doing so, they are a kind of sacrament of Christ. And authentic sacraments bear a natural resemblance to what they signify.

To repeat, though, I don't mean to develop this line of thought here. I wish instead to make certain other points.

One of these is that, although the dynamism driving the campaign for women's ordination originates in feminism, it gets plenty of unintended encouragement from clericalism. That happens in at least two ways.

One concerns a certain idea of Christian life that we consid-ered and rejected earlier—the *realpolitik* view that relationships within the Church, when all is said and done, are a power struggle. In a clericalist system, real power rests ultimately in the hands of clerics (to the extent that some nonclerics have power, it's by way of delegation or power-sharing). In order to obtain and exercise genuine power in the Church, then, you have to be a cleric—that is, ordained. And if women are to have *their* shot at power, women's ordination is essential.

The other way in which clericalism feeds the movement for women's ordination is, I think, something like this. It is a fundamental clericalist assumption that the priestly vocation and lifestyle are normative—they set the standard for all other lifestyles in the Church. To put it simply: the priesthood is the highest expression of the Christian life, the best way for anyone to follow and imitate Christ. If, however, the priesthood is the highest expression of the Christian life, it is an obvious injustice to refuse to allow half of all Christians—women—access to it. A woman who wants to be a superior Christian will want to be a priest; telling her no is transparently unfair.

To be sure, there are answers to these ways of thinking. Life in the Church is not a power struggle but a collaborative venture, based on the equality in dignity of the members and their complementary roles in carrying on the work of Christ. The priesthood is *not* the norm or standard for everyone but only for those whose unique personal vocations call them to it (and the Church's validation, given by those who exercise pastoral authority, is required to authenticate any claim, whether by a man or a woman, to have a priestly call). These principles are of central importance to interpreting the statement of Canon 208 that "there exists among all the Christian faithful a true equality with regard to dignity and the activity whereby all cooperate in the building up of the Body of Christ."

Still, such answers cannot help but remain difficult for some people to grasp and accept as long as clericalist modes of thinking and acting persist. My first conclusion then—and I'm sorry to say it is not very encouraging—is that the controversy over women's ordination to the priesthood won't finally be settled until we have finally settled the problem of clericalism.

Pending that, however, there are things which can be done by women who don't care to be stalemated forever in a bitter wrangle about women's ordination but would rather get on with the work of sharing in the Church's mission to the world.

Clearly, such women do exist. Not long ago a Catholic woman of my acquaintance and her husband had dinner with another couple. The woman, a successful attorney as well as a mother, was livid afterward. "I meet so many women who say they're angry at the Church!" she exclaimed. "Here was another one. When they get talking, though, you pretty soon find out that they're really angry at themselves for not accomplishing more. I'm tempted to say, 'You want a career—want to be a lawyer? These days a woman can do it if she cares to make the effort.' I think that, as a matter of fact, the angriest women I know are the biggest dilettantes." (I'm glad she said it. No man could get away with saying that today.)

In *The Lay Members of Christ's Faithful People*, Pope John Paul insists that lay women, quite as much as men, share in Christ's threefold mission as prophet, priest, and king, and so share in the "fundamental apostolate of the Church"—evangelization. In this Christian work, he says, women are called to use the God-given gifts that are theirs precisely as women.

No doubt the Church, like other groups and institutions in society, was slow in catching on. But now, as the Pope points out, the Code of Canon Law contains numerous provisions on the participation of women in the Church's life and mission, including being members of consultative and decision-making bodies and holding positions in the ecclesiastical administrative structure. Yet even these things, important as they are, do not get to the heart of the matter—namely, the "two great tasks" that Pope John Paul says belong to women today: "First of all, the task of bringing full dignity to the conjugal life and to motherhood... [and] secondly the task of assuring the moral

sion of culture" (*Christifideles Laici*, 51).

What does that mean? Something I read not long ago in *The Washington Post* suggests an answer. Assessing the abortion debate, a *Post* editor—a woman—wrote: "The fact is, abortion right now is being left undefended by its true champions—by the women who owe not their lives, but their lifestyles to the convenience of legal abortion. Yes, convenience."

By way of illustration, she wrote of a friend of hers who a few years back "had herself a summer"—a break from school, a high-paying restaurant job, "lively night life and an older boyfriend." And at the end of it all, "my friend had her abortion, finished her summer, went back to school. Having a baby was never a consideration."

And of another friend, a twenty-seven-year-old woman lawyer, with "a great job and a devoted boyfriend and potentially doting grandparents nearby." She also had an abortion—which she now calls a "non-event"—after landing an even better job.[3]

The abortion issue is symptomatic but not exclusive. Today there is a broad agenda of cultural and social issues, many of them marriage- and family-related, about which men, for better or worse, no longer have any significant say in practice. These matters are the preserve of women. Pope John Paul's "two great tasks" appear to take this reality fully into account. Either committed Christian women themselves will recapture broad areas of contemporary life from advocates of the morality of "convenience" or else that will not happen at all. In this cultural context, I confess, the whole argument about women priests strikes me as rather trivial.

One final word about "women's concerns"—and it concerns men. Pope John Paul remarks that during the 1987 synod on the laity "many voices were raised... expressing the fear that excessive insistence given to the status and role of women would lead to an unacceptable omission"—namely, "the absence or the scarcity" of men from various forms of involvement in the life of the Church (*Christifideles Laici*, 52).

This has always been more or less a problem. Women traditionally have been more "religious" than men, and in some cultures it is almost a point of masculine pride for laymen not to be too visible or active in Church-related endeavors. In the Church in the United States today, perceptive observers worry about what they call the growing "feminization" of religion. Too much emphasis—or the wrong kind of emphasis—on women in the Church can only make this problem worse. While attending to the gender-related grievances of one sex, we must be careful not to give the other an excuse for dropping out.

The Pope suggests that the solution lies mainly, though not exclusively, in recapturing a sense of Christian marriage as a man-woman partnership in vocation. The preservation and strengthening of Christian marriage and family life in the face of a hostile secular culture are tasks of immense and urgent importance. And they are the right and the responsibility, above all, of lay men and women.

4. THE RENEWAL OF THE PARISH

Canon law speaks often of parishes. The parish is the basic, ordinary jurisdictional unit in the Church. More than that, parishes like Holy Family are where most Catholics experience the reality of ecclesial community—supposing, of course, they experience it at all. Catholics traditionally have loved their parishes and been richly nurtured there, both humanly and spiritually. Many can hardly think "Church" without also thinking "my parish."

Parish renewal has been a recurring topic among Catholics in the United States for years now. Several organized "renewal" programs exist, and some report substantial success. Still, there are signs that all is not well with American parishes.

A pastoral letter issued by the bishops in 1992 (*Stewardship: A Disciple's Response*) takes a fairly grim view. "Although religious people often speak about community," it remarks, "individualism infects the religious experience of many persons. Parishes, dioceses and Church institutions appear impersonal and alienating in the eyes of many."

Elsewhere, this document exhorts parishes to "be, or become, true communities of faith." Pastors and parish staff, it says, must be "open, consultative, collegial and accountable in the conduct of affairs." Parishioners are urged to "accept responsibility for their parishes and contribute generously—both money and personal service—to their programs and projects."

Many observers of American parish life have reached similar conclusions and offered like prescriptions. Obviously the description of parishes as alienating and impersonal does not fit every parish in the land. There are many that are true communities of faith. But, just as obviously, the description applies to some. Why is that? What can be done about it?

The problem has a number of causes. One, frequently noted, is that many parishes are just too big. Priests and parish staff and parishioners hardly know one another. People encounter one another as strangers, with few opportunities to develop personal relationships. In such parishes, it is said, even the celebration of the Eucharist can take on the character of a remote, abstract ritual rather than a participatory, community-building action.

No doubt all that is true in some cases. Excessive size can be an obstacle to building and sustaining parish community. Hence, the impersonal and alienating environment of which the bishops speak in their letter.

Other factors also seem to play a role: the isolating geographical configuration of many neighborhoods, demographic differences within parishes, lifestyle patterns including work and commuting that keep people—women as well as men—

out of their parishes during the week and leave them exhausted on weekends. All of these things, and a lot more about the way Americans now live, can and do have a negative impact on parish life in Holy Family and a lot of other places.

These are the sociological explanations, some of them, anyway. But there also is another factor that ordinarily does not receive a lot of attention in discussions of parishes and their problems, yet may do more than all the rest to bring about an atrophying of parish life. It is the erosion of consensus on matters of faith that has taken place among American Catholics over the last three decades.

More than anything else, I believe, this weakening of faith-consensus weakens the sense of religious community in parishes. Despite the superficial calm prevailing in Holy Family Parish, the number of people involved in parish life has dipped steadily in the last two decades, and all is not well just below the surface. No doubt there are a number of reasons, but one reason certainly is the situation we are now considering. If, when all is said and done, Catholics do not share the same faith regarding matters central to Catholic life, there is very little to hold them together for the long pull. Recent sociological studies of mainline American Protestant churches suggest, incidentally, that the same calamity—failure to teach and transmit core Christian doctrine regarding salvation in and through Jesus Christ—befell them earlier and largely accounts for their striking, sad numerical decline over the last half-century.

In a personal letter, Bishop Weigand of Salt Lake City decried this state of affairs as it pertains to a matter of bedrock importance both to the spirituality of individual Catholics and to the unity of the faith community—the Eucharist. Over the last several decades, he contended, what many Catholics were taught about the Eucharist was "watered down and distorted," so that "a whole generation... has been raised with imprecise language and a vague understanding." Now, he said, many such people simply do not grasp the fact that in receiving Holy

Communion, they are "really and truly receiving the body and blood, soul and divinity, of the Lord Jesus Christ, under the appearance of bread and wine."

Is this a problem in only one American bishop's diocese? I regret to say that I doubt it.

I cite the example of declines in knowledge about and belief in the doctrine of the Eucharist only because it is so clear and troubling. Polls and studies of various kinds show that the problem doesn't stop there. Plainly there is widespread confusion about the Church's moral doctrine (sexual morality and much else). Still more alarming in their way are data showing that even many Catholics who attend church regularly either do not know or else do not accept major elements of Catholic teaching. (And what of the huge number of Catholics who rarely or never go to church any more?)

The results are now apparent in parish life in many places. The principal result is a serious fracturing of unity among the members of the people of God. Even in parishes where this situation exists, it is true, persevering Catholics still can find the sacramental roots necessary to nourish their spiritual lives. But the breakdown of authentic community—a breakdown arising in large measure from a breakdown of faith-consensus—seriously complicates even that task.

Canon law (for example, Canon 229.1) affirms the right and duty of lay Catholics to a sound formation in Catholic doctrine as well as the duty of the Church's pastoral leaders to provide it. Yet, as we now recognize, there has been a serious catechetical breakdown in the last twenty-five years. A whole generation of American Catholics has suffered. This points to an urgent need for a vast new effort of catechesis—the teaching of the faith—directed to laypeople of all ages, occupations, and ethnic groups (and not just to the laity either: priests and religious share this need). The new *Catechism of the Catholic Church*—the "universal catechism" sponsored and endorsed by Pope John Paul II, and published in English translation in 1994—provides an occasion.

If we fail to seize the opportunity thus providentially offered to us, this present crisis could end in disaster. We have Jesus' word for it that the Church herself will prevail against the gates of hell and will last until, literally, the end of time. But that is no guarantee that the Church in any particular place—including the United States—will survive a long-continued failure to teach the basic doctrines of the faith with courage and conviction. We can count entirely on God's fidelity, but we cannot presume on him always to rescue us from the consequences of our own folly and neglect.

TEN

Getting Ready to Excerise Our Rights and Responsibilities

THE SUBJECT IS FORMATION for the exercise of our rights and the fulfillment of our responsibilities as members of the Church. How do we as laypeople prepare and sustain ourselves to do what our personal vocations within the communion of faith call for us to do?

It's unfortunate, by the way, that we have to speak of this work of preparing and sustaining as "formation." This is one of those churchy words with no adequate substitute. "Training" suggests regimentation and indoctrination. "Education" implies a largely academic, intellectual activity. "Formation," despite its disadvantages, at least has the merit of indicating an integrated, comprehensive process that takes place on the spiritual as well as the intellectual level and is geared to helping persons make mature, responsible use of freedom.

Strange to say, people commonly undertake some of the

most important commitments in life without much formation in this sense: for instance, marriage and parenthood (which, for most members of the Catholic laity, are central to defining their rights and responsibilities *as Christians*). The assumption appears to be that anybody can be counted on to know, naturally and spontaneously, just what to do—and also to do it—in order to carry out the complex, demanding requirements of being a spouse and parent.

That might have been a reasonable assumption (and then again, it might *not*) in simpler times and more stable societies than ours. In other eras—perhaps—spousal and parental roles were clearly defined. Children ordinarily were "formed" by the good example of level-headed, loving parents. The surrounding community, in turn, offered substantial encouragement and support to families, while the Church's worship and catechesis could be counted on to spell out the moral and doctrinal dimensions of things. Then, perhaps, the neglect of formal formation was not so risky, considering that an informal but apparently effective *de facto* system of formation was at work.

It's not that way any more. In a typical parish like Holy Family dysfunctional as well as single-parent families are common, even among churchgoers. Children growing up in such homes may lack sufficient exposure to sound models of domestic life to guide their own standards and behavior as husbands and wives, mothers and fathers. And the secular culture is in a never-ending state of radical confusion about gender roles, relationships in marriage, and much else with a bearing on family life, while routinely manifesting extreme hostility to traditional views on such matters.

Popular media catering to the young—television, movies, music—are filled with nihilistic yet seductive messages about love and sex, parenting and marriage, the value of human life, and ultimate purposes and meaning. (MTV, it has been said, is engaged in "cynically ripping off the idealism of youth and repackaging it for resale to Budweiser." And, at times, even the representatives of the Church appear to have difficulty formulating—to say nothing of communicating, in the face of a hostile secular din—the Christian message on these matters. Monsignor Hellman and Father Ross struggle manfully, but in their hearts they sometimes suspect it's a losing battle.

To say that planned, organized, comprehensive, continuing *formation* for marriage and parenthood is needed in these circumstances is to state the obvious.

But not just for marriage and parenthood. The whole broad range of roles that Catholic laypeople are called upon to carry out today, precisely in their capacity as members of the Church—along with the rights and responsibilities that accompany these roles—requires a serious approach to formation on the part of all concerned.

Otherwise, it seems fair to say, talk about rights and responsibilities in the Church is meaningless at best and at worst can undermine authentic communion by fostering a power-struggle mentality or encouraging the clericalization of laypeople through overemphasis on ministries. If the day of "pray, pay, and obey" is over and done with—if Catholic laypeople now are entitled (as well as obliged) to see themselves as partners of bishops, clergy, and religious in carrying on the mission of the Church—they must seek and receive a great deal more formation than many now commonly seek or receive.

What should this formation look like? It has at least three aspects.

First, there must be a significant doctrinal component. In his document on the laity, Pope John Paul speaks of the "ever-increasing urgency" that Catholic laypeople learn the content of the faith in order to give effective Christian testimony to a skeptical secular society. That is especially the case for laity engaged in the professions and in public life. "Above all, it is indispensable that they have a more exact knowledge...of the

Church's social doctrine." That requires, the pope adds significantly, "a more widespread and precise presentation" of social doctrine than is now common (*Christifideles Laici*, 60). I have already spoken above of the need for doctrinal formation in discussing parish life and its renewal and will not repeat here what has been said.

Second, formation for vocational discernment. This is a critically important and widely neglected requirement. We need to take a close look at what it means.

Third, spiritual formation—the cultivation of the interior life in an authentically *lay* mode. It is an inescapable fact that, as Pope John Paul II says: "The vocation of the lay faithful to holiness implies that life according to the Spirit expresses itself in a particular way in their involvement in temporal affairs and in their participation in earthly activities" (*Christifideles Laici*, 17). Laypeople must learn how to become saints in, not apart from the secular world.

Let us take a closer look at number two and number three.

A QUESTION OF VOCATION

Near the end of his apostolic constitution on the laity, Pope John Paul makes a statement that is likely to strike not a few people as surprising and, perhaps, bordering on the incomprehensible. "The fundamental objective of the formation of the lay faithful," he writes, "is an ever-clearer discovery of one's vocation and the ever-greater willingness to live it so as to fulfill one's mission."

When you come to think of it, that is a profound remark. It implies several things of great importance.

One implication is that vocational discernment is as necessary for those whom God calls to be laypeople as it is for those called to the priesthood or the religious life. There is a revolution in Catholic thinking in that.

Many of us who attended Catholic schools or simply listened to Sunday sermons some years ago can recall periodically being exhorted to think about vocations. The meaning was, in a way, admirably clear: "Does God want you to be a priest or a nun? Give it some thought." There was and is absolutely nothing wrong with that. The possibility of such a call is something virtually every Catholic *should* consider at some time (or even many times) in the course of his or her life. Yet this way of putting the question frames vocational options too narrowly. For laypeople also need to discern their vocations *as laypeople*. It is just as simple—and as complicated—as that.

A second implication of the Pope's words is that, while deciding on a *state in life* is part of vocational discernment, so also is the discerning of a *unique personal vocation*. In fact, we might say, it is the latter which provides the framework for the former: state in life is *part* of personal vocation. Indeed, as Pope John Paul says, it is "personal vocation and mission" that define "the dignity and the responsibility of each member of the lay faithful." For "from eternity God has thought of us and has loved us as unique individuals. Every one of us he called by name" (*Christifideles Laici*, 58).

A third implication is that it is necessary not only to discern a personal vocation—to see what God asks of one—but to accept that calling and live it out. This, obviously, is not something done once and for all. It is a lifelong, day-in and day-out task. "Only in the unfolding of the history of our lives and its events is the eternal plan of God revealed to each of us.... It is a gradual process; in a certain sense, one that happens day by day" (*Christifideles Laici*, 58).

And a fourth implication, among others which could be mentioned, concerns our rights and responsibilities as members of the Church. Only by discerning, accepting, and trying to live out our unique personal vocations can we really know, in concrete practical terms, what these are. Canon law and

Church teaching lay down general principles and norms, and these are both valid and important as far as they go; but personal vocation brings them to life for each Christian.

MAKING DEMANDS ON THE YOUNG

American children have many problems. It would be foolish to suggest that they are all reducible to only one, for the confusion and perversity of adults have produced a luxuriant variety in the forms of neglect and abuse of the young. Even so, certain broad patterns of malfunction and misguidedness do stand out. One of these resides in the fact that, often enough, nobody expects very much of children.

Parents who are uncertain about value and meaning in their own lives, or simply too busy and preoccupied to care, ask nothing of their offspring except that they stay out of trouble (at least, the kinds of trouble that might be troubling to them). Schools burdened by the consequences of parental and societal neglect—as well as by their own mistakes and evasions—praise and promote students whose performance is, by any realistic standards, mediocre or even worse. Even churches and religious education programs preach to the young a message of easy grace and redemption without the cross—a feel-good religion of self-affirmation that troubles consciences (if it troubles them at all) only on behalf of causes deemed politically correct.

The results are predictable. Children of whom little is expected tend to expect little of themselves.

Of course there are exceptions—thank God, quite a few. Encouraged by prudent adults, a substantial number of American young people continue to internalize values and make worthwhile commitments. They are high-minded, hardworking, and idealistic. May their tribe increase!

But there are other children and young people, tragically many, of whom this is simply no longer true. Instead of meaning, there is an enormous vacuum, a great emptiness, in their lives. Like any other vacuum, this one sooner or later does get filled: by sex, drugs, and violence in some cases; status-seeking and consumerism in others. A cynical and exploitative media youth culture (concocted by adults who aim to profit from pandering to the immaturity and weakness of the young) papers over the emptiness with glitz and false glamour. The disturbingly high incidence of teenage suicide and other forms of self-destructive behavior supply a kind of sinister static in the background, audible beneath the stereo thump of rock and rap.

Where nothing much is asked or expected of children, the stage is set for trouble. Sooner or later, reality can be expected to assert itself, with disastrous results. As I write this, the papers and the TV news are full of stories about a fourteen-year-old boy in the nation's capital who shot and seriously wounded a school security guard. The youth is said to have had a problem with authority, and the unfortunate guard represented authority for him.

An extreme case, no doubt. Yet not, essentially, all that unusual. A child on whom no demands have been placed regarding discipline and self-control is likely to rebel and lash out—if not with a concealed handgun, then in some other way—when, finally, someone or something does make a demand.

It is a mistake to think of this as a problem of race or social class. The children of affluence and comfort manifest this pathology in their own particular way. The late Allan Bloom offered a devastating portrait of them in his much-discussed book *The Closing of the American Mind,* and others have done the same. The point made by critics like Bloom is that these well-to-do young Americans in many cases lack any significant convictions or commitments—except, of course, a commitment to themselves and their own self-interest, narrowly understood. It is a deeply troubling charge that in many instances rings all too true.

Unfair? Yes, if taken as a picture of all well-off American young people. No, as a description of many.

FORMATION FOR VOCATIONAL DISCERNMENT

For the Church at least there is a solution within reach. Yet this solution still is not commonly recognized as such, even by those who might be expected to do so. The solution to the vacuum of meaning and commitment otherwise existing in the lives of children of whom little is expected or asked is personal vocation. It is also the key to rights and responsibilities in the Church. Children and young people have vocations. They must be taught that they do, and helped to find out what their vocations are.

The clericalist notion that "vocation" refers *only* to a calling to the priesthood or the religious life is a major obstacle. Even today it persists and is reinforced in many ways.

"Vocations" directors, "vocations" offices, "vocations awareness" programs—what are these? Generally speaking, they are personnel, offices, and programs that try to encourage people to enter the priesthood or religious life. And of course people should be so encouraged. The problem is not that there's something wrong with fostering priestly and religious vocations. The problem is that understanding vocation only in this way overlooks the fact that everyone without exception has a unique personal vocation to be discerned, accepted, and lived out. Unless that fact is underlined, chances are good that those not called to the priesthood and religious life will conclude (having never been told differently) that they do not have vocations at all, while those who really do have callings to these special forms of Christian service may never realize the fact.

The fostering of vocations awareness in its comprehensive sense should begin very early. It must start in the home, as something parents routinely do with and on behalf of their children.

There are many theories of child development. It is not my intention (even if it were within my competence) to endorse one or another of them here. I only make the common-sense observation that all developmental theories concur that children grow up in fairly well-marked stages (allowing for individual variations from one child to another), so that the education and formation of children should proceed accordingly. This is applicable to the question of forming children for vocational discernment, as well as for the exercise of their Christian rights and responsibilities.

Start with the very young.

In the case of very young children (let us say: ages three or four to seven or thereabouts) "formation for vocational discernment" plainly doesn't signify heavy-handed pressure to choose a vocation or anything like that. Very likely the abstract and mysterious word "vocation" should not even be used.

Instead, the process of formation should be spontaneous and perfectly natural, a part of the way the family lives. Young children are quite able to grasp the idea that they have duties and obligations—things their parents and other responsible adults rightly expect them to do (and not do). It is not difficult to teach them that they have genuine duties to other people—brothers and sisters, playmates and schoolmates, parents and themselves. "Helping out" in the family through the regular performance of simple chores is a good way of doing that. So is the routine observance of reasonable family rules about things like meals, bedtimes, and getting up on time. Lest there be any doubt, these things *are* elements—very important ones—of the personal vocations of young children right here and now.

God also should be part of the vocational formation of the very young. Do not teach: "God is a stern policeman waiting to punish you if you get out of line." Do teach: "God is a loving Father who has done much for us and to whom we owe much in return."

Regular family church attendance, regular family prayer, regular reception of the sacraments (Communion and Penance) by parents as well as by children, participation in parish social and religious events—all these help make the point that God and the Church expect something of us. So does gentle but repeated instruction in the fact that God's expectations, and our duty to live up to them, extend to every-day things like homework, keeping one's room and clothing in reasonably good order, obeying parents and other responsible adults, treating friends with respect and consideration, and making up with them after a quarrel. For children, such instruction not only is training for the discernment of a voca-tion at some point in the more or less distant future—it is prac-tice in living out a real though still-developing vocation right here and now.

And that undoubtedly is the point that requires special emphasis in the case of children who are somewhat older—from seven or eight, let's say, until twelve or thirteen: "You have a personal vocation here and now." In most cases, its components are reasonably clear. Family and church, school and neighborhood—these are not just environments where children enact certain roles and perform certain tasks. More importantly, as the child experiences them, they are inter-personal communities, networks of relationships, involving sig-nificant responsibilities and rights. The sum of these relationships, with their accompanying rights and duties, in each case *is* a personal vocation.

Even at this age, but especially as they move into the teenage years, children also should be introduced to this fur-ther thought (not in just these words, however, but in lan-guage they will understand):

Not so very far in the future, it will be necessary for you to begin considering those long-term choices and decisions that will permanently shape the rest of your life. It is extremely important for you to think of these in vocational terms. The central question is what God wants *you* to do. Is he calling you to the priesthood or religious life, or to the state of a layperson in the world? To marriage or the single life—perhaps as a member of an apostolic movement or sec-ular institute? If to marriage—then marriage to whom?

What kind of work or profession does God wish you to pursue? Where?

No one else will be able to make these decisions for you, although, if you are wise, you will seek advice from others. And the decisions should not be made in haste or simply in response to strong (and possibly temporary) feelings. Nor should you decide simply on the basis of what you think *you* would like to do—what will give you the greatest immediate gratification as that is measured by some limited standard like income or prestige or pleasure.

The challenge instead will be to learn what God is asking of you and then make a generous response, since that is how to achieve real happiness. It will take time, and some false starts are possible along the way. But it is none too soon to start the process and to keep the question—what does God want of me?—before you. Keep it before you as you go about doing many of the things that you will naturally do over the next several years: studying, dating, even daydreaming about the future and trying out possible careers and lifestyles in your imagination. Never doubt for a minute that God does have something in mind for you. A great deal of your vocation at this stage of your life, and also for some time to come, consists in learning what that is.

Decent and concerned adults naturally want the young people for whom they are responsible—their daughters and sons, their students, their young parishioners—to be happy. That certainly is true of the priests and people of Holy Family Parish. But for various reasons, ranging from personal shyness to culturally-conditioned confusion about the meaning of personal autonomy and the nature of personal happiness, many such adults today seem more or less reluctant to speak to young people in these vocational terms. That, unfortunately, also is true in Holy Family.

Canon 219, with its caution against coercing people in

choosing a state in life, provides no warrant for this reluctance. Certainly there should be no force or manipulation in this matter. But telling children and young people that they soon will have important choices to make, and that these choices should be shaped by what they see God wants of them, is *not* coercion. It is an important exercise of parental duty in regard to the young, as well as that of other adults who bear some responsibility for the child.

Persons familiar with today's young people often remark on their hesitancy to make serious, long-term commitments. Fear of commitment is cited as an explanation for the dropoff in the numbers choosing the priesthood and religious life, as well for parallel phenomena, like the startling rise in those who experiment with "living together" before marriage (if they marry at all) and the substantial increase in the average age of those marrying for the first time. If young people have problems making commitments, though, one reason may be that adults—parents, teachers, pastors—have failed to tell them that they have personal vocations, that these personal vocations involve lasting commitments, and that playing fair with God requires that they work hard at discerning their vocations and making the necessary commitments.

A LIFELONG TASK FOR EVERYONE

Pope John Paul, taking a realistic view, remarks that for every person there are certain "particularly significant and decisive moments" for discerning God's call and responding to it, and that, for most, adolescence and young adulthood are especially critical times in this regard. But he also points out that discerning and accepting a personal vocation are not tasks for adolescents and young adults only. On the contrary, the Lord "calls at every hour of life so as to make his holy will more precisely and explicitly known" (*Christifideles Laici*, 58).

That also makes perfectly good sense when you think of it.

The large, long-term commitments (state in life, job, or profession, and so on) are the frameworks within which we realize our unique personal vocations; but within those large and often somewhat stylized frameworks, individuals have to make countless choices and decisions about *how to live out* the commitments in response to the concrete, daily circumstances of life. The large commitments, we might say, are the skeletons of people's personal vocations upon which the here-and-now choices about how to live them out put on flesh and blood.

This is hardly a novel thought. In his spiritual classic *Abandonment to Divine Providence*, the seventeenth-century French Jesuit Jean Pierre de Caussade speaks of what he calls "the sacrament of the present moment." Where, he asks, do people find God's will for them? In the actual circumstances of their lives here and now—in the tasks and duties of their various states of life, that is, and also in the kaleidoscopic variety of needs and demands encountered in daily living.[1]

De Caussade does not use the language of unique personal vocation, but he is referring to essentially the same thing. God calls us at each moment, in the duties, joys, and trials that moment brings. "Therefore," Pope John Paul says, "the fundamental and continuous attitude of the disciple should be one of vigilance and a conscious attentiveness to the voice of God" (*Christifideles Laici*, 58).

It sounds simple, but anyone who tries it soon learns that it isn't. Most of us tackle our days with set ideas concerning what we mean to accomplish—finish this project, start that one, make these phone calls, set up those appointments, go here, go there, do this, do that. It is good and necessary to plan one's day, organize one's time, so as to be productive and get things done—including the doing of God's will. But it also is necessary not to set one's own ideas about what needs doing ahead of God's ideas on the subject. It is possible to be so insistent on doing something (even something good) that we have chosen, that God's call goes unheeded.

What we intend to do may or may not coincide with what God really wants. When circumstances make it clear that we cannot accomplish something we have in view (a flat tire prevents me from keeping a business appointment, a rainy day disrupts a family's plan for a picnic in the park), then it is we who must change and not God. The "sacrament of the present moment" puts things in proper order by inviting our watchful attentiveness to God's will as it manifests itself in the events of everyday life. It is a key by which we can see what our rights and responsibilities really are here and now.

But the key won't work without our constant efforts to dispose ourselves to use it. To be sure, God sometimes does intervene very dramatically in people's lives, making his will for them crystal clear. St. Paul on the road to Damascus is an example of that, and many other persons have had conversion experiences of their own, even if less dramatic ones. More commonly, though, God speaks quietly, without much fuss—almost in conversational tones, as it were. His voice is not inaudible, but we must tune out other noise.

A SPIRITUALITY OF RIGHTS AND RESPONSIBILITIES

Seeking God's will and doing it are not activities carried on in a vacuum. Grace is indispensable. Grace aside, the practice of discernment and fidelity is only possible in the long run within the context of a plan of life and a spirituality. For laypeople, naturally, this means developing and cultivating a *lay* spirituality.

Whatever else this expression "lay spirituality" may mean, it does not mean a second-rate spirituality, a watered-down spirituality, a form of spiritual life for lazy, half-hearted, and distracted Christians, a compromise solution for people who want to get to heaven without breaking a sweat. The Second Vatican Council, in its *Constitution on the Church*, reminds us of God's "universal" call to holiness—a call, that is, directed to all. Lay men and women, it says, are summoned to the perfection of charity—they are called to be saints.

A genuinely lay spirituality nevertheless does have a distinctive character. Call it, for lack of a better name, secularity. Not *secularism* but *secularity*, the special note of life in the secular world.

The joys and griefs, the triumphs and tribulations, of this way of life—the tensions and fulfillments that are part of marriage and family life, the pain and the satisfaction of hard work, study, recreation, and friendships, of health and sickness alike—all these things, along with prayer and participation in the sacramental life of the Church, are the means, the instruments, of lay sanctity.

That finally is why the Council speaks so strongly against the "split" between faith and life. It is why Pope John Paul warns against trying to lead "two parallel lives"—the weekend churchgoing life of a Christian on the one hand and, on the other, the weekday life of a man or woman immersed in the world, with each "life" lived in isolation from the other according to its own particular set of priorities and norms (See *Christifideles Laici*, 59). Each of us lives one life and one life only. That life in its totality is our path to God.

Let's consider briefly what that means in regard to two matters of central importance in the lives of the vast majority of people, whether or not they have their eyes set on becoming saints. I mean marriage and work.

MARRIAGE AS A WAY OF SANCTITY

Not so long ago I saw a Steve Martin movie called *Father of the Bride*. (People of my generation also will recall an earlier version starring Spencer Tracy.) It's the story of a family caught up in preparations for their daughter's wedding. Not a bad film, generally speaking (except for a casual attitude toward premarital sex—par for the course these days, unfortunately) and surely not a movie meant to be taken very seriously. Yet something about the film, apparently taken for granted by those who made it, set me thinking.

This is the story, I repeat, of people preparing for a wedding. Not a *marriage*—a *wedding*. There's a world of difference. The *wedding* preparations depicted in the film were lavish and exhaustive. The preparation of the young couple for *married* life was non-existent (or else it was happening somewhere off-screen—it played no role at all in the story). Here, I thought, were two kids who no doubt loved each other, immaturely but genuinely, yet were stumbling into life together with nary a thought for what comes after the honeymoon.

From that perspective, this modest comic fantasy was telling a deeply serious story repeated time and again in real life. Countless young (and not-so-young) people really do devote vast amounts of time and energy (and money) to getting ready for their weddings but, consciously at least, give almost no attention to marriage preparation. It's a risky mistake whose results can be disastrous.

Even in human terms, it's obvious why that is so. Throw a non-swimmer into the pool and will he swim? Sometimes, maybe, but what sensible person wants to risk it? Throw two romantically involved people into the state of matrimony, and will the result be a permanently bonded couple able to weather the strains that are sure to come? Sometimes, yes; very often, no.

Membership in the communion of faith, the Church, both enriches and heightens the challenge of marriage. Canon 226.1, expressing the Church's wisdom in legal terms, reminds married Catholics of their duty to "work for the upbuilding of the people of God through their marriage and their family." This is no trivial obligation. On its fulfillment depends "success" in Christian marriage itself. Is everybody getting ready for a wedding automatically up to fulfilling what the canon calls a "special duty"? Do I hear someone saying, "Interesting point—but excuse me, I have to call the caterer now"?

For many years the Church has offered marriage preparation programs for couples getting ready for marriage, and in many places participation in such a program is required for those who wish to be wed "in the Church" (receive the sacrament of matrimony, that is). In recent years, too, numerous dioceses in the United States, recognizing the extremely strong likelihood that a premature and hasty marriage will fail, have insisted that persons under a certain age observe a waiting period of some months before receiving the sacrament. (Obviously, if such people are of legal age to be married, they can proceed immediately to a civil marriage regardless of what the Church says. In that case, however, they are not sacramentally married— they are not married in the eyes of the Church. They are committing objective sin and they are ignoring sound advice based on much practical experience.) Such provisions and requirements on the Church's part are prudent and good.

What message do people preparing for Christian marriage (and perhaps also those who prepare people who are preparing for Christian marriage) most need to hear today? Obviously, many important messages need to be communicated at this time: about the responsible use of sexuality in the service of life and love according to the teaching of the Church; about generous acceptance of the children whom God may send; about acquiring and practicing a realistic Christian attitude toward money and material possessions so as to avoid that spiritual deathtrap called consumerism; about the complementary roles and equal dignity of man and woman in marriage; about the centrality of faith and religious practice in happy and healthy families. That's a lot of ground to cover!

But something else comes first—something that draws everything else together in a coherent pattern. It is that Christian marriage is a *vocation*.

The marriage of Christians has this character of vocation in two ways.

First, because sacramental marriage is a state in life or Christian lifestyle—one of those large-scale, overarching commitments (religious life and priesthood are others) that serve to organize and set the course of the lives of those who make them. Vatican II speaks of marriage as a vocation in this sense, and it is now common for papal and episcopal teaching documents to make the same point.

Second, because the commitment to the marriage state and to all that it entails by way of duties to spouse, children, and the community at large (including, as Canon 226.1 points out, the community of faith, the Church) is a critically important element in the unique personal vocations of those Christians who make it.

It would be difficult to exaggerate the practical importance of this vocational view of marriage.

Many people today understand marriage more or less exclusively in terms of *self*-satisfaction and *self*-fulfillment, as one more way of getting what *they* want out of life. Popular culture—television, movies and the rest—give steady, powerful support to this attitude. When two people who think like this wed each other, their marriage is essentially a contractual arrangement allowing mutual exploitation. Children tend to be viewed the same way. These people want to be parents because parenting will fulfill them, or else they avoid parenthood because children would get in the way of something else they want more: career, travel, an affluent lifestyle, whatever it may be.

We have here what might be called the sitcom vision of marriage and family life. It's terrific as long as it's fun, but it's a drag when the fun stops. No doubt some people always have approached marriage in this spirit, but the individualism—the radical emphasis on "what's in it for me?"—that pervades contemporary American culture causes it to be both widespread and entrenched at the present time.

Needless to say, this way of thinking can be, and very often is, fatal to marriages. For when a marital relationship stops being fulfilling (in the sense in which people who think like this understand fulfillment: as a steady, unbroken stream of gratifying experiences for them), when personal differences and incompatibilities surface, when sickness and tension and fatigue rear their ugly heads—when, in short, the going gets rough, as sooner or later it does for every married couple—then such people must either begin to grow up together by adopting a mature ideal of *mutual* fulfillment, or else they will almost certainly throw in the towel and split. Many split.

The sense that one's marriage—*this* marriage, to *this* other person—is part of a unique personal calling from God is an antidote to all this. In some cases, people come to understand their marriages this way as part of their experience of married life itself. More power to them! They have learned what fulfillment in marriage is all about.

Ideally, though, it is desirable for people to acquire this vision of marriage long *before* the wedding. Early adolescence, when dating has hardly begun and courtship still lies somewhere in the future, is the time for teachers and pastors and parents to introduce young people to the idea that marriage, for those whom God calls to it, is a central part of their vocations. As that suggests, marriage preparation understood as a conscious, deliberate exercise in vocational discernment must begin a lot earlier than is commonly recognized. The "Pre-Cana" class may be ten or fifteen years too late!

Much more could and probably should be said about the actual living of Christian marriage as a part of personal vocation. And, as a matter of fact, much of it already has been said by Pope John Paul in his beautiful 1981 document on *The Role of the Christian Family in the Modern World*. (Its Latin title is *Familiaris Consortio*.) It is not easy reading, but it contains much wisdom. Get it, read it, discuss it with others—your boyfriend or girlfriend, your fiancé, your spouse, other couples. It will repay the effort it requires. Here, though, it's time to move on to a second major dimension of a truly secular lay spirituality: ordinary work.

A SPIRITUALITY OF WHAT?

Back in chapter eight we looked briefly at work as one of the areas in which, Pope John Paul says, Catholic laypeople are meant to make their special contribution to reforming and renewing the world. What is involved might be called the "humanizing" of work—in other words, doing what lies within one's power to make ordinary work a source of authentic fulfillment for oneself and others. That is idealistic and difficult, no doubt, but it also is urgently necessary.

Now our focus is more specifically upon work as an element in the spiritual life. ("Work" incidentally is not synonymous with "job." For a student, for example, "work" means studying. For a full-time housewife, it's household duties. In other words, "work" is the form of activity—paid or unpaid, onerous or agreeable, as the case may be—by which a particular person makes a contribution to meeting his or her daily practical needs and the needs of others.)

At this point, though, we immediately encounter a problem. Most people spend many hours a day thinking about the work they do as well as actually doing it. But far fewer, it seems, approach their work as a bonafide element in their spiritual lives.

Instead, starting out in life, young people tend to think of work simply as a way of getting ahead and getting what they want—an outlet for their energies and ambitions, an activity with a monetary or emotional payoff down the line. This is not wrong in itself, yet it is uncomfortably limited and limiting to those who hold such a view. Moreover, it is likely sooner or later to end in frustration and bitterness for those who fail to develop a more mature attitude. Life has ways of seeing to that.

That began to dawn on me a while back, as, more and more frequently, I encountered what at first struck me as a strange phenomenon. Quite a few of my friends, contemporaries of mine, were conspicuously unhappy in their work and didn't mind saying so. They'd been passed over for promotions they felt they deserved. They were stuck in routine and (by now) meaningless jobs. They weren't getting the recognition and respect they craved. They were too young to retire and too old to change. (Accurately or not, one of my friends confided that people in his office had begun to think of him as the "old fart.") They were fed up and permanently disgruntled. They wanted out.

It would be naïve and insensitive to imagine that a person who finds himself or herself in such a situation doesn't have a problem. The question is: What to do about it? Become a chronic complainer? Drink more than you used to do? Run off to Tahiti and take up painting? Or start thinking about work from a spiritual perspective? Before doing any of the other things, I suggest giving the last a try.

Here's one way.

Some years ago Pope John Paul wrote an encyclical called *On Human Work*. Like many of his writings it is difficult reading, but it is worth the trouble. He says work has two Christian meanings that are central to the spiritual life. For someone who once begins to take them seriously, they can make a big difference.

The first of these meanings is "co-creation." My apologies if that seems at first glance to be a pretentious and obscure word, but it sums up the idea better than any other term available. To be sure, only God is the creator, in the sense of bringing things into being out of nothing. Yet, having created us human beings, God invites us to join him in this activity—to cooperate with him in realizing his creative plan.

This is clear in the case of what we call procreation, where human parents cooperate with God in the begetting and nurturing of new human beings. Procreation brings a man and woman as collaborators into God's own laboratory of life—an awesome role.

But human collaboration with God does not stop there. We

cooperate with God in bringing new aspects of reality into existence all the time, and the most obvious way is through our work. That is so not only of so-called creative work—painting, sculpture, music, writing, the performing arts, as well as science and technology—but also of quite ordinary, even humdrum, forms of endeavor. Honorable, honest work of any kind, no matter how seemingly humble it may be, builds up the world as God intends. It is "co-creation." God *could* do it all, but in fact he leaves a lot to us.

The second Christian meaning of work identified by the Holy Father is what is called "co-redemption." Once again it is necessary to be clear about what is meant. Only God redeems—we are not saved by our own good works, as a modern-day Pelagian might suppose. But as with creation, so with redemption, God invites us to cooperate in the process by which we ourselves and others are redeemed.

Central to that process is the cross and what it stands for: fidelity to God's will that turns aside at nothing, not even one's own suffering and death. Occupying as it does this central place in the divine plan of redemption, the cross also gives meaning to the experience of human suffering that is joined to the redemptive suffering of Christ. "I rejoice now in the sufferings I bear for your sake," St. Paul exclaims, "and what is lacking of the sufferings of Christ I fill up in my flesh for his body, which is the church" (Col 1:24).

That should not be misunderstood. I remember making the same point another time in something else I wrote, and getting a stinging letter from a nurse who works with oncology patients. She chewed me out for suggesting (as she thought) that the best advice for people suffering great pain is, "It's God's will—offer it up." "Easy for you to sit at your typewriter and pontificate," she wrote.

Of course, that is not what I am suggesting. It is a great Christian ministry to prevent human suffering whenever it can rightly be prevented or else alleviate it when that is possible.

And yet, in this life, not all suffering can be prevented or alleviated. Then what are those who suffer supposed to do? The Christian answer is: will to unite the suffering with the redemptive suffering of Jesus Christ.

That applies to what is painful and unpleasant, both physically and emotionally, about work. In itself, work is not a punishment for sin, and it would be wrong to suppose otherwise. In the Genesis account, God places the first man in the Garden of Eden "to till it and to keep it." Work was necessary to human happiness and fulfillment *before* the fall (Gn 2:15).

As a result of sin, nevertheless, work did become burdensome in many ways ("By the sweat of your brow you shall eat bread," God tells Adam in Genesis 3:19). It is burdensome now and always will be. Fatigue, frustration, disappointments, failures, setbacks, rebuffs, unjust criticism, unpleasant bosses, uncongenial fellow workers, long hours, inadequate pay, the sense that what one does is futile or unappreciated, the aches of heart and body that can come with work—all these present an opportunity for co-redemptive suffering with Jesus Christ.

No more than I would counsel someone suffering physical pain to "offer it up" would I advise a worker who is having a hard time in work to be merely passive and take it on the chin. The advice being offered here is significantly different. Do what you reasonably and responsibly can to make your work rewarding in every way. But when you experience unpreventable and unremovable suffering in connection with work—as, almost certainly, you sooner or later will—choose to make this an act of co-redemption in cooperation with Christ. Join it with the cross by a conscious and deliberate act of the will, for your own spiritual benefit and the benefit of others.

CONCLUSION

There is so much else that can and should be said about the spirituality of the laity—about the sort of interior life by which lay men and women living and working in the world can respond to Vatican II's universal call to holiness and become canonizable saints! I cannot say it all here. In fact, it has been said, and said much better, by others, among them St. Francis de Sales, Blessed Josemaria Escriva, and Pope John Paul II. The most glorious right and most solemn responsibility of laypeople is to be saints.

Now, though, it is time to draw this discussion of the rights and responsibilities of the laity to a close.

Plainly this has not been a comprehensive, technical treatment of canon law. As I said at the beginning, that was not my aim. I've tried instead to focus on certain central themes of the 1983 Code that shed light upon important duties and rights of laypeople as members of the Church. The most important of these is summed up in one word: holiness.

These duties and rights do not ultimately come from canon law, however. The Church's law calls attention to them, recognizes them, gives them a certain institutional status, but it does not create them. They come from the very nature of the Church and from membership (in its fullest and deepest sense) in the communion of faith that is the people of God and body of Christ. More immediately, they come from the ecclesiology—the vision of this Church of ours and Jesus Christ's—that underlies the great teaching documents of Vatican Council II.

In our times, the equal dignity of laypeople as members of the Church has again been fully recognized, after a lapse of many centuries. So have the right and responsibility of the laity to do their share in carrying on the mission of the Church, which is the mission of Christ, in and to the secular world. This is not properly the work of bishops and priests and religious. If Catholic laypeople do not do it, it will for the most part not get done, and they and the Church and the world will all be the losers. This message has been slow to sink in, not just in Holy Family Parish but in most other places in American Catholicism.

But why look at it in that negative light? In reality, as far as rights and responsibilities of the laity are concerned, we Catholics have taken giant strides in a very short time. The message *is* starting to be heard.

Now why not go the rest of the way?

Notes

FOUR
Canon Law and the People of God

1. Jordan Aumann, O.P., *On the Front Lines* (Staten Island, NY: Alba House, 1990), 48.

FIVE
Obligations and Rights of the Laity

1. Alvaro del Portillo, *Faithful and Laity in the Church* (Shannon, Ireland: Ecclesia Press, 1972), 125.

SIX
Rights versus Responsibilities?

1. Cormac Burke, *Authority and Freedom in the Church* (San Francisco, Calif.: Ignatius Press, 1988), 111.
2. John Finnis, "The Foundations of Human Rights," *Catholic Position Papers,* July, 1992, 1.
3. Finnis, "The Foundations of Human Rights, 2."
4. Finnis, "The Foundations of Human Rights, 2."
5. Germain Grisez, *The Way of the Lord Jesus,* Vol. 1, *Christian Moral Principles* (Chicago, Ill.: Franciscan Herald Press, 1983), 121-122.
6. Finnis, "The Foundations of Human Rights, 4."
7. Finnis, "The Foundations of Human Rights, 4."
8. Grisez, *The Way of the Lord Jesus,* 271.
9. Grisez, *The Way of the Lord Jesus,* 273.
10. Grisez, *The Way of the Lord Jesus,* 123-125 and 135-136.
11. Grisez, *The Way of the Lord Jesus,* 270.
12. Grisez, *The Way of the Lord Jesus,* 671.
13. Germain Grisez, "Vocation in Family Catechesis" in *The Church and the Universal Catechism* (Steubenville, Ohio: Fellowship of Catholic Scholars, 1993), 152.

SEVEN
The Problem of Clericalism

1. See Russell Shaw, *To Hunt, to Shoot, to Entertain: Clericalism and the Catholic Laity* (San Francisco, Calif,: Ignatius Press, 1993).
2. John Henry Newman, "Contest between Faith and Sight" in *A Reason for the Hope Within* (Danville, N.J.: Dimension Books, 1985), 115.

EIGHT
Laity in the World

1. George Weigel, "The Future of the John Courtney Murray Project" in *John Courtney Murray and the American Civil Conversation* (Grand Rapids, Mich.: William B. Eerdmans Publishing Company, 1992), 284.
2. Christopher Lasch, "'Good Enough'—The American Way" in *Providence: Studies in Western Civilization* (Fall, 1992), 12.
3. Stanley Rothman, "Religions Bad Press" in *First Things* (January, 1994, no. 39), 9-12.

NINE
Four Special Problems

1. John Henry Newman, *On Consulting the Faithful in Matters of Doctrine* (New York: Sheed & Ward, 1961), 106.
2. Germain Grisez, "The Right to Be Educated—Philosophical Reflections," in *The Right to Be Educated* (Washington, D.C.: Corpus Publications, 1968), 64.
3. Carolyn Hax, "No Birth, No Pangs" in *The Washington Post* (March 21, 1993) sec., "Outlook," 1.

TEN
Getting Ready to Exercise
Our Rights and Responsibilities

1. See Jean Pierre de Caussade, *Abandonment to Divine Providence* (New York: Doubleday/Image Books, 1975), 51.